PRINCESS ANNE AND MARK PHILLIPS
TALKING ABOUT HORSES
With Genevieve Murphy

Princess Anne and Mark Phillips – Talking About Horses

with Genevieve Murphy

Hutchinson/Stanley Paul, London

Hutchinson/Stanley Paul & Co Ltd
3 Fitzroy Square, London W1

An imprint of the Hutchinson Publishing Group

London Melbourne Sydney Auckland
Wellington Johannesburg and agencies
throughout the world

First published 1976
© Genevieve Murphy 1976

Set in Monotype Bembo

Printed in Great Britain by
The Anchor Press Ltd, and bound by
Wm Brendon & Son Ltd, both of
Tiptree, Essex

ISBN 0 09 128090 7

Contents

INTRODUCTION   7

1 Early days   9
2 Mark and Rock On   15
3 Princess Anne in training   23
4 Mexico and Haras du Pin   27
5 Doublet, Purple Star and Chicago   34
6 Success at Badminton   42
7 A European title   47
8 The Munich Olympics   55
9 Columbus and Goodwill   61
10 Disaster in Kiev   67
11 Triumph and tragedy   75
12 Columbus at the World Championships   80
13 An all-female team   85
14 The Road to Montreal   95
15 The Montreal Olympics   102

APPENDIX I: The event horses ridden by Princess
Anne and Mark Phillips   108

APPENDIX II: Records   113

GLOSSARY   117

ACKNOWLEDGEMENTS   122

INDEX   124

Introduction

When I first set off for Sandhurst to talk to HRH The Princess Anne and Captain Mark Phillips about their horses and their sport, I was naturally apprehensive. I had taken two tape recorders rather than one, so that the recurring nightmare of a totally blank tape might have less chance of becoming a painfully embarrassing reality. I had also taken a sheaf of notes, with the mistaken idea that this would be more of a formal question-and-answer session than a lively discussion.

It was delightful to be proved so totally wrong. The notes were quickly discarded as the Princess and Mark warmed to their theme. In retrospect, it was ridiculous to imagine that two people who have proved their dedication and their courage in such a demanding sport should talk about it in a restrained and formal way. They are, in fact, articulate and entertaining; they are also refreshingly honest when analysing their own performances.

'I'm afraid we do tend to go on a bit when we start talking about horses,' said the Princess, as I prepared to leave. It was a tendency for which I was heartily grateful.

I am hugely indebted to Princess Anne and Mark Phillips for their co-operation. To have the opportunity of hearing the private background story behind their public achievements in three-day eventing was a very great privilege – and I only hope that I have done it full justice.

My grateful thanks are also due to Mark's parents, Mr and Mrs Peter Phillips, and his trainer, Bertie Hill, to Princess Anne's trainer, Alison Oliver, and to the British chef d'équipe Colonel Bill Lithgow. They have all helped me to tell the story of the Royal couple and their horses.

GENEVIEVE MURPHY

1 | Early days

'I must have been very young at the time,' said Princess Anne, 'but I have an impression of one very large grey cob and two rather small grey ponies, all of them plaited and absolutely spotlessly white from head to foot. Miss Sybil Smith was on the cob in the middle, Charles and I were on either side on the ponies. We were both on a leading-rein and we were *towed* around a cinder ring, but the fastest we ever went was a trot. I'm afraid I thought it was a most grisly waste of time.'

She had been disenchanted from the moment the leading-rein was produced, for she already considered herself to be beyond that stage. In fact it was a source of childhood pride that she came off the leading-rein before Prince Charles, who is almost two years her senior.

The Princess, who was born on 15 August 1950, was too small when given her earliest riding lessons to remember much about them now. The same applies to her husband, whose less publicized birth had taken place on 22 September 1948, and who was something of an infant equestrian prodigy since he was happily riding on his own from the age of four.

Apart from the spotless plaited pony (which she rode at Sybil Smith's establishment at Holyport, near Maidenhead) the Princess's early association with ponies was probably similar to that of any other small child born into a horse-loving family. 'One was presented with a small hairy individual and, out of general curiosity, one climbed on.'

Meanwhile, Mark Phillips had been presented with a small hairy Shetland called Tiny Wee and had actually won his first rosette, in a leading-rein class, before the age of two, at about the time that Princess Anne was born. 'When one is very young,' he said, 'one doesn't really have much say in what the pony does – but I suppose it's the beginning of getting a basic seat that becomes natural to you.'

His mother, who led him round the ring in those early days, had taught him to ride by using an appropriately simple line of instruction: heels down, hands down, sit up, look up – 'and it actually used to work for about half an hour!'

A broken arm, sustained when he fell off his second pony, Longdon Beauty, at the tender age of four, made no apparent inroads on Mark's confidence. He was only six when he progressed to a 13.2 pony called Pickles, while Longdon Beauty continued the rounds of local leading-rein classes with Mark's sister, Sarah, in the saddle. By the time he was seven, Mark was hunting Pickles regularly and jumping quite sizeable fences.

Princess Anne, though denied the chance of hunting during her childhood, was far from confined to sedate hacking when she rode with the Queen in the wide open spaces of Windsor Great Park. 'We had one splendid mare,' she said, referring to the Royal ponies who had as much character and as many wayward inclinations as anyone else's ponies. 'She was solid concrete from the neck backwards and she permanently ran away; one could pull for all one was worth but it made absolutely no impression. Luckily, she always stopped before she got to a fence or a road, so it never used to worry one. I was really extraordinarily lucky with the ponies I had. They were by no means saints and they didn't do all the things they were told to do, but they taught me a tremendous amount.'

Mark had occasional braking problems as well. A family friend remembers him, while out hunting as a very small boy, screeching to his mother because he couldn't stop. 'Well, what on earth do you want to stop for anyway?' asked Anne Phillips as they thundered on. It took a few moments for the question to sink in. Then Mark's brow cleared; he was out hunting and he wasn't really the least bit interested in stopping, so he relaxed and enjoyed himself.

It was, perhaps, a fairly typical example of his mother's outlook;

she is warm and womanly and gently humorous, but she is certainly no mollycoddler. And neither is her husband, Peter Phillips, who firmly believes that competitive riding ('and hunting is competitive in a way') is the best incentive for any small boy to work at his riding.

So Mark hunted; he went to shows, gymkhanas and hunter trials; he took part in the rallies and competitions organized by the Ledbury branch of the Pony Club which he joined at the age of five. When he was eight, he rode Pickles at Badminton, in one of the working pony classes that used to be held in conjunction with the three-day event. It was a competition that he was to win on two subsequent occasions, both of which involved the excitement of receiving the winner's prize from Her Majesty the Queen. Little did he know that he was then making the acquaintance of his future mother-in-law.

As Mark says himself, it was always 'made easy' for him to ride. Plenty of other parents have been left to bleat at their sons, whose ponies seemed to be permanently in the field and never ridden. Anne Phillips, anxious that riding should be a pleasure rather than a chore, caught Mark's pony herself and tacked it up. The enthusiasm, built up during those early competitions and while hacking around the family farm near Tewkesbury, was to lead him towards an intense interest in stable management in his own good time.

Princess Anne, who says she could probably count the number of junior competitions she took part in 'on the fingers of one hand', was a member of the Garth branch of the Pony Club – and so was Prince Charles. Since they were usually at Sandringham for Christmas and at Balmoral during the summer, their Pony Club activities, however, were restricted to the Easter holidays.

The Princess was the more actively involved. She had outgrown her first pony, and its successor, a roan mare called Greensleeves, had developed laminitis and had been retired to stud. So her partner was an elderly grey pony called Bandit, who had carried other children through their early Pony Club days before being lent to the Royal Family – and he had acquired a mind of his own. 'Once he'd done one bending race,' said Princess Anne, 'he wouldn't do another. It was the same with show jumping. He'd do one round but if you wanted to go into the ring again you had to back him in.'

Mark also acquired an elderly partner for Pony Club competitions. His name was Rocky, formerly owned and show jumped by the Duke of Norfolk's daughter, Lady Sarah Fitzalan Howard, whose aunt had married Mark's uncle. Having graduated to horses, Lady Sarah was to win the individual title in the 1959 Junior European Show Jumping Championships at White City, where she was also a member of the victorious British team.

Rocky arrived when Mark was nine, shortly after the Phillips family had moved to their present home at Great Somerford, which is mellow and comfortable and homely. The move involved changing from the Ledbury to the Beaufort branch of the Pony Club – and it was to have far-reaching effects since it gave Mark the opportunity of training under two Olympic riders, first Colonel Alec Scott and then Colonel Frank Weldon.

Colonel Scott chose Mark, then aged only twelve, for the Beaufort Pony Club team which he was training for the 1960 Championships. It was, in retrospect, a most illustrious team for the other three members were Jennie Bullen (now Mrs Loriston-Clarke and Britain's leading dressage rider). Mike Tucker, who (like Mark) has since become an international three-day event rider, and George Weldon, whose father was an Olympic gold medallist.

It wasn't, however, a happy beginning for Mark. He was riding his recently acquired 14.2 hands pony Archer, with whom he achieved a splendid dressage score, only to be eliminated for three refusals at the water during the cross-country phase – 'It's been the same all through my life: when things have been going well I've gone *woomph* straight back to the bottom again!'

'His mother says it's good for his character,' said Princess Anne. 'So I keep telling him he must have a very strong character by now!'

The Princess experienced similar problems with her 14.2 pony, High Jinks, to whom she graduated at the age of eleven. 'He was only four when we got him, so we pottered along together for a

while and then we did a few competitions. He was marvellous
in every respect except that he wouldn't jump a ditch unless he
was in company.'

High Jinks, competing in hunter trials, was therefore better
in pair classes than in individual events. 'Except,' said Princess
Anne, 'that they had an awful habit of building fences of three
different sizes and I was usually sent round on the outside where
they were highest. It wasn't the line I'd have chosen if I'd been
jumping on my own!'

The elimination of Mark's Archer was not in the least characteristic for he was probably the best schooled and most obedient
pony to arrive at Great Somerford. He was followed by Pirate,
who was bold and brave but so sensitive that he had to be ridden
as though the reins were made of silk, and then by Kookaburra,
who required constant pushing.

'More by accident than by design,' said his mother, 'Mark was
fortunate in that the horses he rode were all completely different
so that he had to change his way of riding for each one of them.
This, in the end, is what goes to make the horseman.'

Mark was equally fortunate in his instructors: Alec Scott and
Frank Weldon in the Pony Club, and Molly Sivewright, of the
Talland School of Equitation, to whom he went for extra tuition.
Despite the elimination he was chosen to ride for the Beaufort
Pony Club for another four consecutive years and he reached the
finals on three occasions, once with Pirate and twice with Kookaburra. There was an additional glamour to the finals at that
particular stage in that they were held at Burghley, on the day
after the three-day event, and included some of the renowned
cross-country fences – such as the Trout Hatchery, which the
Pony Club riders jumped in the opposite direction to their seniors.

After a few years with Alec Scott, who taught him a great deal
about dressage and show jumping, Mark and the other members
of the Beaufort Pony Club team were instructed by Frank
Weldon, a team gold medallist in the 1956 Olympics and now
Director of the Badminton Horse Trials. Frank's forte was the
cross-country and it is no coincidence that some of his former
pupils went on to prove their worth in a bigger pond. Apart from

Mark Phillips and Mike Tucker, they included Jane Bullen (now Mrs Holderness-Roddam), who had followed in the footsteps of her sister Jennie and was to become the first woman to win an Olympic three-day event medal.

At that stage, Mark was at school at Marlborough where his sports were rugger and athletics, while riding was confined to the holidays. Princess Anne, however, had the advantage of having High Jinks with her during one whole year of her schooldays at Benenden. The pony was stabled at the Moat House Riding School next door to Benenden and, according to the Princess, 'he had more instruction there than he'd ever had in his life – and so did I.'

Riding round a school was not Princess Anne's idea of bliss but she had, by then, decided that it might be beneficial: 'One had to put up with it because there might be something to be gained in the long run.' She had no idea in which direction she wanted that 'something' to take her and the instructors, around whom she circled, were probably equally unaware of the path she would eventually choose.

She didn't compete in her first Pony Club one-day event until after leaving school, though she had taken part in the initial stages of one that was snowed off. 'I remember doing a dressage test in the snow and the judges couldn't even see me. That was a one-day event that never quite made it.'

2 | Mark and Rock On

Mark's first adult one-day event, at Everdon in Northampton-shire, also took place in a swirl of snow – but this one did make it to a wintry finish. 'I don't remember the dressage or the show jumping,' he said, 'but I do remember that I lost my iron before the first cross-country fence and that I finished the course in a snowstorm.'

He was riding his Pony Club partner, Kookaburra, and he finished in fourth place. A silver ashtray at the Phillipses' home records the spendid consistency of 'Kookie' in novice one-day events that season: 4th Everdon, 6th Sherbourne, 5th Stocken-church, 2nd Wylye, 1st Tweseldown, 1st Mixbury. But when he reached the intermediate grade his limitations were exposed. He was a quality cob, ideal for novice one-day events but lacking the scope or the speed to go any further. After one attempt at an intermediate class, he reverted to hunting at which he excelled.

Kookaburra was owned by Mark's aunt, Flavia Phillips, who has always helped and encouraged him. She also lives in Great Somerford and, over the years, she has provided grazing and stabling, assisted in getting his horses fit for three-day events and helped to transport them to their various venues in her horsebox, which was much more spacious than the Land Rover and trailer belonging to Mark's parents.

Kookaburra's achievements had fired Mark's enthusiasm for eventing and his parents therefore set out to find a replacement. The search led them to Walter Biddlecombe (the father of Terry) and to a six-year-old 16.1 hands gelding called Rock On, whose sire was the Irish stallion Black Rock. The horse changed hands. and in the autumn of 1966 moved to Great Somerford.

'He was a mad devil when we bought him,' said Mark.

'Then why on earth *did* you buy him?' asked Princess Anne.

'I suppose because Walter Biddlecombe, who was selling him, told us that he would jump round Badminton – and in our innocence we believed him! He was quite cheap, but then all our horses were cheap because we couldn't afford any more.'

In fact, Mr Biddlecombe senior was quite right in his forecast, but a few problems had to be ironed out before Rock On proved the point. He was headstrong, impetuous and hopelessly uncontrollable out hunting; so much so that one prospective customer, who had been looking for a hunter, had previously returned Rock On to Walter Biddlecombe as unridable.

Though he clearly had a big jump in him, Rock On's style was on occasion distinctly original. 'He used to go straight up and straight down, just like a flying bedstead,' said Mark's mother. 'But he was incredibly brave; I think he must have been the bravest horse that ever looked through a bridle.'

Mark had just finished school when Rock On arrived and he had some time to spare before he was due to follow in the footsteps of his father, a former Major in the King's Dragoon Guards, by joining the Army. It was therefore arranged that he and his horse should spend four months with Bertie Hill, who was a member of the same three-day-event gold medal team as Frank Weldon, and had since become the official trainer of the British team.

Mark had been to him once before with Kookaburra. 'Frank Weldon sent him to me when he was still in the Pony Club and told me that he could possibly make a very high-class rider. There was never any doubt about that; he was a natural horseman.'

Bertie now runs a highly successful training establishment at his Devonshire farm in South Molton, where he has turned out about as many top three-day-event riders as Eton has turned out Cabinet ministers. When Mark and Rock On went to South Molton, in the January of 1967, he was quick to recognize that the horse also had enormous potential. 'He had tremendous scope,' said Bertie, 'and he was very, very brave; the only real problem we had was in relining the brakes.'

The defective brakes were very much improved by March when the new partnership appeared at the Crookham Horse Trials for their first competition. 'We won a section of the novice,' said Mark, 'and Rock On knocked my two front teeth out! We were about two or three fences from the end of the cross-country, just galloping along on the flat, when he suddenly jumped what must have been a tyre track or a rut. He knocked my two front teeth straight back into the roof of my mouth so, when I finished the course, I stuffed them back in again.'

'It's not surprising that they fell out a few years later,' said Princess Anne.

'No, they didn't fall out, they simply died! The roots took again but the teeth slowly went blacker and blacker, so eventually I had to have them crowned.'

By that time there was already a waiting list for the novice class to be held at Liphook the following week, so Mark decided to ride Rock On in the Intermediate section instead. He finished second in the higher grade and, since the grading system was then worked on a prize money basis, Rock On became an 'Open' event horse within the space of four days.

The Army Horse Trials, staged a couple of months later at Tidworth, were to give both horse and rider their first taste of a full-scale three-day event – and it wasn't (on the face of it) a particularly nice taste since Rock On fell at the second cross-country fence and again on the flat when his suspect brakes caused him to run out of road on a corner. The second obstacle was a brook, followed by two large steps cut into the uphill bank; the horse, who was afraid of nothing, decided that the whole thing should be jumped in one and he paid the inevitable penalty of his own impetuosity. But for Mark, who remounted and completed the course, the error merely highlighted the extraordinary courage of his inexperienced horse; it was therefore a source of wonder rather than a source of gloom.

Mary Gordon-Watson and Cornishman V, also having their first taste of three-day eventing, underlined their combined talents more conspicuously by winning the same novice section of the Tidworth Horse Trials. Rock On had, however, won

B

himself a staunch circle of admirers. Mark's parents can remember being 'absolutely staggered' when, during the summer of 1967, Bertie talked about the horse as an Olympic prospect, for it was before Rock On had even attempted the more rigorous tests of Burghley and Badminton.

Mark's Army career began the same year and September 1967 was to be memorable on two counts: it marked his entry into Sandhurst and his first appearance among the contestants for the three-day event at Burghley. An immediate problem was that Sandhurst rules did not allow a new cadet to leave the grounds of the Academy for his first three weeks, which in this case included Burghley. But Bertie Hill had forewarned Colonel Bill Lithgow, the chef d'équipe of all British three-day-event teams since 1965, that this very promising rider was coming to Sandhurst and must obviously (at least in the eyes of those concerned with eventing) have the chance to compete at the autumn's major three-day event.

Colonel Lithgow was then commanding a College at Sandhurst. Seeking to avoid any embarrassment – or, worse still, any possibility of refusal – he arranged for Mark to be posted to his College and promptly sent him off to Burghley, confident that it would pass unnoticed. It would almost certainly have done so had Mark not finished fourth, with which happy tidings the Commandant's daughter, glancing through the paper the next morning, regaled her father at the breakfast table. A hasty check of this hitherto unknown name and the plot was out!

'Needless to say,' said Colonel Lithgow, 'though all the correct noises were made, it was taken in the greatest possible good part and Mark most handsomely repaid it by ending his time at Sandhurst as Senior Under Officer.'

To go back a bit, the scoreboard at the end of the dressage phase gave no possible cause for alarm; it even, in fact, questioned whether Mark's journey was strictly necessary, for he and Rock On were then almost fifty points behind the pillar-to-post leaders, Lorna Sutherland and Popadom.

But fast clear rounds on the steeplechase and cross-country courses were to give Rock On the maximum time bonus as it then was (nowadays it would have been a zero time penalty) and he moved up to tenth place at the end of the speed, endurance and cross-country phase. In fact, the horse had travelled at such enthusiastic speed across country that he was, incredibly, a full minute under the time for maximum bonus.

Mark had carried a stop-watch on the steeplechase. With two straightforward circuits of the course, it was easy to establish the exact half-way mark; the watch could therefore be used in order to find out whether he needed to accelerate for the second circuit.

But he didn't wear it for the cross-country. 'Personally, I don't think there's any point. Even if you knew exactly where the half-way mark was on the cross-country, it wouldn't bear any relation to the time. The time factor is governed by the fences – if you have open galloping fences you'll go across a piece of country much faster than if you have, say, a coffin or a quarry.'

Another dramatic advance was to be made the following day when only eight of the thirty-three survivors jumped clear show jumping rounds, so that the final phase exerted far more than its usual influence. With one of those eight clear rounds Mark and Rock On moved up to fourth place.

Lorna Sutherland retained her lead to win on the corky skew-bald, Popadom, whose appearance had never remotely suggested that he might have succeeded in winning even a minor three-day event. Since his dam had once pulled a cart in the Lancashire seaside resort of Morecambe, the *cognoscenti* were equally un-impressed by his breeding. It was therefore amusing to see Popa-dom confounding the theorists by winning from a field which included riders from Ireland, the United States and Japan.

The selectors, however, were probably paying more attention to the better-bred horses who followed the skewbald home. These were Althea Roger-Smith's Questionnaire, who was subsequently sold to Canada, Jane Bullen's Our Nobby, Mark Phillips's Rock On and Major Derek Allhusen's Lochinvar.

Ex-members of the Beaufort Pony Club no doubt studied the results and noted with supreme satisfaction that their one-time fellow members, Jane and Mark, had finished in third and fourth places. But Princess Anne doesn't remember even glancing through the results: 'I didn't start competing until the following year and I wasn't really in the least bit interested – I hadn't begun to think of eventing as a sport to be followed.'

In any case, the Princess enjoys the role of participant rather than spectator in equestrian sports: 'I'm not a good spectator of certain things. I don't particularly enjoy going racing, for instance, because when I see all those nice horses I feel I'd like to be riding them. But I can sit and enjoy other sports.'

'If it's good enough,' said Mark. 'Anything less than top class tends to be rather boring.'

'But then it's quite good to watch the bad people, because they show you what *not* to do.'

The Princess started training with Alison Oliver at about the same time that Mark was preparing for his first Badminton. He had been a spectator every previous year, from the time of the inaugural Badminton of 1949 when the crowds were so sparse that he could be left to picnic by a fence with his nanny while his parents walked the cross-country course. Over the years Mark's idea of competing at Badminton moved from the realms of fantasy into a positive goal. 'I suppose it must always have been at the back of my mind,' he said. 'We used to go and watch Badminton and, to begin with, I used to look at the fences and think: *Crumbs!* But eventually it became more of a reality and one thought that it might be possible.'

By the age of nineteen his first Badminton had become part of the natural progression, an automatic next step along the path that had already led him from the Pony Club Championships, via one-day events, to Tidworth and Burghley. With the Olympic Games in prospect, the 1968 Badminton was by no means regarded as an end in itself. The fourth place at Burghley, allied to the knowledge that Rock On possessed phenomenal courage and scope, had engendered the hope that Mark might earn a ticket to Mexico later that year.

His participation at Badminton meant that the organizers had to find a new timekeeper for the cross-country since Mark's father, in charge of the stop-watches for the past decade, would be too involved in Rock On's effort to fulfil his usual role. The horse had spent most of the three-month training period at South Molton, where Bertie Hill took charge of his preparation until Mark was free to join him. Fortunately Sandhurst then had terms, in the same way as a university, so the final training and Badminton itself took place in the Easter vacation, at a time when even the Commandant was perfectly happy for his cadets to be on leave!

And it was a happy leave for Mark. Though slightly short of work, through having struck into himself during his pipe-opening contest at Crookham (injuring the back of his foreleg with a hind foot), Rock On tackled the cross-country course with his usual enthusiasm and moved up from overnight twentieth into third place. He slipped back to fourth on the final day with one fence down in the show jumping.

'There was a difficult treble in the show jumping,' said Mark. 'It could either be jumped with one very long stride between each element or two short ones. A number of horses had been doing it in single strides – and if there was ever a horse that should have done that it was Rock On. But, foolishly, I asked someone who didn't really know the horse for advice and, as a result, I tried to take two strides each time, which was how we collected ten penalties.

'You have a problem when you're young, because you haven't the experience to know what the hell you should do. You get wiser as the years go on, but the trouble is by the time you have the experience you may have lost some of the dash! There's no question about it, you don't bounce as easily after a certain age.'

The 1968 Badminton was another triumph for the former Beaufort Pony Club team, for Jane Bullen won the Championship on the small and marvellously gallant Our Nobby, defeating two members of Britain's Tokyo Olympic team – Richard Meade on Turnstone and Staff-Sergeant Ben Jones on Foxdor. Derek All-husen and Lochinvar, destined to cover themselves in glory before the year was out, finished close behind Mark in fifth place.

The top five at Badminton – among them Mark with Rock On – had earned their place on the Olympic short-list that was

announced a few days later. The others were Fiona Pearson with
Ballinkeele, Lorna Sutherland with Nicholas Nickleby and Martin
Whiteley with The Poacher. Richard Meade was the only rider
with two horses – Turnstone and Barberry – among the Olympic
candidates.

The short-list seemed to represent an embarrassment of riches
for the selectors, but it was to become sadly depleted before the
team of four riders and the reserve boarded the aeroplane that was
to take them to Mexico.

3 | Princess Anne in training

While the selectors were deliberating over the 1968 Olympic short-list, Princess Anne was having her first lessons with Alison Oliver. She had been preceded to Warfield by Purple Star, owned and bred by the Crown Equerry, Colonel Sir John Miller, who had sent the horse to Alison with the idea that the Princess would eventually ride him in her first one-day events. He was, in fact, the second of Sir John's horses to arrive at Warfield – but the first, Blue Star, was considered by Alison to be unsuitable 'for starting a teenager off in eventing'. With a down-to-earth practicality that has been much appreciated by her Royal pupil, Alison didn't distinguish between starting a teenager and starting a Princess.

Purple Star, then only five years old, was the son of Sir John's former three-day-event mare, Stella, with whom he had finished seventh in the 1951 Badminton Championships. Stella had been lent to the British team for the 1952 Olympics in Helsinki (where Mark Phillips's future trainer, Bertie Hill, rode her into seventh place) before she was retired to stud. Happily, her ability was passed on to Purple Star.

In retrospect, Princess Anne's first appearance at Alison's stables seems to have been remarkably well timed. 'I was presented with Purple Star and more or less told to get on with it,' said the Princess. 'There wasn't any conscious choice about it. But, though I'd probably have gone on hacking around quite amiably, I was beginning to feel that I'd like to do something else. I'd have been quite happy (if I'd been given the chance) to have had a shot at playing polo because it was something different, and I'd watched it since the year dot and always enjoyed it; I think it's a very good game.'

In addition to watching Prince Philip and Prince Charles play polo, the Princess had watched the Badminton Horse Trials 'from the year dot' – but she doesn't consciously remember doing so. 'I used to go when I was really small but then, when I went to school, it was slightly interrupted – and there were two years running when everyone else went off to Badminton and I was left behind with either chickenpox or measles. So I didn't go for three or four years, until I started competing.'

The path towards competing at Badminton began at Easter time in 1968, when she began riding Purple Star under Alison Oliver's tuition. It was to prove a breakthrough from elementary horsemanship into all the more advanced subtleties that the average weekend rider never has the opportunity to comprehend. Nuances in the use of hands, legs and seat; appreciation of a horse's balance, suppleness and cadence, all had their part. 'I could obviously manage a horse,' said Princess Anne, 'but I didn't really know much else. It was Alison who managed to communicate what it was that the horse should be doing, and how to achieve it. In my experience, that is a very rare accomplishment.'

Alison, who had been able to train Purple Star without any inhibitions, admits that it wasn't quite as easy – initially at least – to yell instructions at a Princess. 'I suppose that I was a bit self-conscious in the first instance, but it was literally only for the first two or three lessons and then I got over it. If you're teaching somebody to ride, you have to fall into a relationship; in fact it's the easiest way of getting to know someone because you are on mutual ground.'

The Princess was, according to Alison, 'fairly passive to begin with. In a way that's often a very good start; it meant that she was relaxed and that she didn't have any adverse effect on the horse. The most difficult people to train are those who are very stiff and rigid, because then you have to try and stop them doing something that they don't realize they're doing. But Princess Anne was always very relaxed (and, if anything, rather ineffectual) so there was something positive to build on, rather than something

Mark on Longdon Beauty at the age of four ('I suppose it's the beginning of getting a basic seat'). Princess Anne, aged nine, on Greensleeves ('I was really extraordinarily lucky with the ponies I had'). *Below:* At eleven, in a working pony class on Pickles with Jane Bullen, now Mrs Holderness-Roddam, next in line.

Prince Charles, with Princess Anne on the 14.2 hands pony High Jinks – 'He was only four when we got him so we pottered along together.'

OPPOSITE PAGE: *Below:* Mark on Pirate, who was bold and brave but very sensitive. The Princess at a polo match ('I'd watched it since the year dot and always enjoyed it'). Princess Anne takes off Greensleeves' bridle while the Queen holds William.

Mark on Kookaburra in his first adult one-day event – 'I finished the course in a snow-storm.'

Below: Princess Anne on her first event horse – 'I was presented with Purple Star and more or less told to get on with it.'

Mark and Rock On in the 1969
European Championships at
Haras du Pin. 'I went swanning
in thinking "this is an easy
fence" and we turned upside
down.'

Alison Oliver keeping warm in the
Royal horse rug (*above*) and discussing
one of the 1971 Badminton fences
with Princess Anne, who 'didn't
expect to get round'. But get round
she did, in magnificent style, on
Doublet (*right*).

OPPOSITE PAGE: Mark and Chicago
III at the 1970 World Championships
('he went absolutely brilliantly until . .
. . .')

Below: The winning British team
(left to right): Richard Meade on
The Poacher, Mark on Chicago III,
Stewart Stevens on Benson and Mary
Gordon-Watson on Cornishman V,
with their chef d'équipe, Colonel
Bill Lithgow.

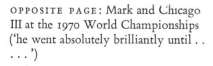

Mark at Badminton in 1971, on the way to achieving the first of his two consecutive victories with Great Ovation, who 'jumped a reasonable round but there was nothing very brilliant about it'.

Below: Princess Anne on Royal Ocean with the Queen, Prince Philip and Alison Oliver.

that one had to stop her doing. And she did have this natural balance and relaxation, which is so terribly important.'

Anyone who imagines that Princess Anne insists on plushy comfort and all its trappings is fundamentally and comprehensively wrong. Her Royal birth and upbringing haven't turned her into a super-deb; she has her feet planted more firmly on the ground than many of her mother's subjects. And she certainly doesn't swan around waiting to be waited on.

'If we were moving jumps around,' said Alison Oliver, pointing to the windswept field where she trains her pupils and where her international show jumping husband, Alan, trains his horses, 'I promise you that Princess Anne would hump as many fences about as anyone else. She's quite willing to take on the really grotty jobs and, if she feels they need doing, she'll put her back into them. Nothing's too much trouble for her.

'In fact, I thoroughly admire her in every way. There have been times when she's been riding that I know I've worked her hard, but she'll never complain. Even if she's not feeling well, she'll keep going; she doesn't let any physical discomfort stop her, whereas an awful lot of people decide that they've got a bit of a headache and give up. If Princess Anne didn't happen to be feeling well, I'd never be told about it; she wouldn't think of using it as an excuse for not riding well. I think this is something that goes to make the really good competitive rider.'

Though Alison wasn't born within sight of a silver spoon, it is easy to understand how she hit it off with her Royal pupil. Both are hard-working, direct and articulate; both are totally devoid of either twee sentiment or petty snobbery. And both had the greatest regard for Purple Star, through whom they first met. 'We were very lucky with Purple,' said Alison, 'he was particularly gifted and he taught Princess Anne a tremendous amount.'

He was not, however, particularly angelic and some of the lessons he taught her may have been a trifle painful. 'I remember having a lovely time, whizzing round the cross-country course of a Pony Club one-day event,' said Princess Anne, 'until we came to a fence that was built between three trees. Purple shied at a Land Rover and ran down the fence; I hit the middle tree and somehow managed to finish sitting underneath him. When I returned, Colonel Miller told me (rather kindly) that I would have won if I hadn't fallen off. And that's been the story of my life!'

'Rubbish,' said Mark, quite rightly.

4 | Mexico and Haras du Pin

Princess Anne and Purple Star made their eventing debut at Eridge in the August of 1968. It was not a debut that Mark would have been able to pinpoint but another of the Olympic short-listed riders, Jane Bullen, can recall it instantly.

She and her sister Sarah were staying with friends for Eridge and they both nearly fainted clean away when they heard, on the Friday morning, that the Queen would be among the guests for dinner that evening. But it turned out to be a marvellously happy, relaxed evening and the Bullen sisters, with their irrepressible vitality and total lack of affectation, were soon their normal, natural selves.

Sarah began going into gruesome details about the cross-country course to be jumped the following day when it suddenly dawned on her that Princess Anne would be taking part. So she stopped in mid-sentence and said cheerfully to the Queen: 'Oh, I'm not worrying you, am I? I'm sure Princess Anne will be quite all right.' At which everyone collapsed into laughter.

Sarah's prediction was correct. Princess Anne was indeed quite all right and she finished fifth in a novice section that was confined to riders under the age of twenty-one.

Meanwhile, Mark was involved in the more exalted advanced class, in which some of the short-listed riders were appearing for the first time since Badminton. Rock On, not yet fit, was an absentee but Mark had the ride on Pollyann Hely-Hutchinson's The Lavender Cowboy, who had been loaned to the British team, and he rode him into fourth place. The winner was Sheila Willcox, riding Fair and Square, who had been omitted from the

Olympic short-list but was clearly intent on making the selectors think again.

Rock On had, at the request of the selectors, undergone a hobdaying operation earlier that summer and his preparations for the autumn then had to be fitted in with Mark's commitments as a Sandhurst cadet. It was at Sandhurst that Mark was telephoned from Canada, by the Canadian team trainer, and asked whether he would sell the horse. The price mentioned initially was £5000, which was a princely sum in those days, and it was later found that the Canadians would have gone a lot higher. At that time it seemed like a fortune to Mark but the question, when put to his father, was quickly resolved.

'Money alone does not buy Derby winners,' said Peter Phillips, 'nor does it buy three-day event horses of Olympic standard. You may fall between two stools, but equally you may never have another chance. So the horse is not for sale.'

Sadly, Mark did indeed fall between two stools. Rock On's operation had meant that there was desperately little time to get him fit for the three-day event at Burghley which was designated the final trial for the Olympic candidates. 'There really wasn't enough time to get him fit,' said Mark, 'and nowadays one would never even attempt it. But unfortunately we tried and he broke down.'

Rock On was found to be lame on the evening after his final gallop and it was naturally a bitter disappointment. He was by no means the only short-listed horse to drop out that year: Foxdor died from a heart attack; Barberry broke two ribs and a bone in his pelvis when falling on the cross-country course at Burghley; Turnstone went lame.

There was a good deal of juggling after Burghley, where Sheila Willcox had won again with Fair and Square, and the selectors eventually named their team for the Olympics: Derek Allhusen on Lochinvar, Jane Bullen on Our Nobby, Richard Meade on Cornishman V (whose usual partner, Mary Gordon-Watson, was nursing a broken leg) and Ben Jones on The Poacher, whom Martin Whiteley had lent to the team. Mark Phillips, to his pleasure and surprise, was chosen as reserve.

'I was dead lucky to go to Mexico,' he said. 'Initially, I suppose, I'd got on to the short-list through my own merits by finishing fourth at Badminton but, when Rock On went lame, that seemed to be the end of it. The selectors first asked Sheila Willcox to be the reserve, but she said that she would only go to Mexico as a member of the team. So then they asked me and I jumped at it.'

In those days only one reserve was allowed between all three equestrian competitions and, according to Peter Phillips, 'considerable amusement was had in speculating on Mark having to stand in for a sick dressage or show jumping competitor'.

Sheila would almost certainly have felt frustrated to be in Mexico preparing for an event in which it was highly unlikely that she would have the chance of competing. But Mark wasn't in the least frustrated – 'I knew I didn't have a dog's chance of competing and that's probably why I enjoyed it so much!' In fact, the 'dog's chance' nearly came up when Richard Meade pulled his rib muscles during some swimming pool larking and was in serious danger of having to miss the Olympic contest.

The selectors had come in for a good deal of pasting when their team was announced. Equestrian journalists, myself included, were quick to point out that neither Richard Meade nor Ben Jones had ridden their Olympic mounts in a single competition beforehand. It seemed, we all maintained, a crazy time to try and begin welding two new partnerships. Yet, with the wisdom of hindsight, it would be difficult to disagree with Mark's assessment: 'They were four great horses; it was probably the strongest team that any country has ever produced.'

But there was a moment when that team might not have arrived in Mexico in full. As Lochinvar was being led into a crate before being hoisted into the aircraft, he ran back and lost his bridle. For what seemed an age he stood free with nothing to stop him careering off into the vastness of the airport and the hazards of the runways. Without a word being said grooms, officials and supporters, who had come to see the horses off, moved into a circle around him. He was rebridled and the moment of crisis was past.

The deluge on cross-country day in Mexico is now legendary.

Mark was on the steeplechase course, sending back information to the team, when the rains came. 'There was water everywhere,' he said. 'It was running down inside one's shirt and inside one's trousers.' He had paddled his way to the cross-country course by the time Ben Jones and The Poacher, last to go for the British team, splashed through the flooded fields to complete a clear round under atrocious conditions. Richard Meade, jumping when the rain was beating down in its full fury, had also gone clear on Cornishman V – and so too had Britain's pathfinder, Derek Allhusen, whose sterling performance with Lochinvar was to give him the individual silver medal and a place in the sporting headlines, which invariably described him as either 'the Galloping Major' or 'the fifty-four-year-old grandfather'. Jane Bullen ('the Galloping Nurse') was the only British rider to have incurred jumping penalties. Our Nobby had fallen twice, through no fault of his own but because his forelegs had sunk into deep mud on the landing side of two fences and he was unable to extricate them in time. But Jane had completed the course and she eventually finished in eighteenth place.

Mark was naturally there to see the British team receive their gold medals and, equally naturally, he joined in the celebrations which ended with a party at Prince Philip's villa, where everyone had the chance to cool off in a floodlit swimming pool. It was a wonderful end for a wonderfully united team. 'Certainly it was one of the happiest teams that I've been associated with,' said Mark.

Though he had shared in the celebrations, Mark was still awaiting the first opportunity to ride with the Union Jack on his saddle-cloth. When he returned from Mexico his sights were therefore set on the European Championships to be held in France the following year. Rock On wasn't ready to contest the 1969 Badminton Championship, but his name still figured on the European Championship short-list which was announced soon afterwards. Mark was eventually chosen to represent Britain as an individual.

His first trip to France during 1969 had, however, nothing to do with three-day eventing. He went to Saumur, the home of the

French cavalry, during July in order to compete in a steeplechase in which officer cadets from various different European countries had been invited to take part on borrowed horses.

'I thought it would be more like a cross-country race or a glorified hunter trial,' he said, 'but I arrived there to find a proper racecourse, with a paddock and a tote and a proper number board. I hadn't bothered to do anything about my weight and they were all riding at something ridiculously low, like ten stone. It was dreadfully embarrassing to find that I was almost two stone overweight, especially when it went up on the board!'

He nevertheless won the race and his parents still have the silver cup to prove it. 'The only reason I won,' said Mark, 'was because the horse being ridden by the other cadet from Sandhurst ran out; instead of going round a U-shaped bend, he went straight on towards the stables. He was in front of me at the time and, when his horse ran out, he carried two very good Italians out with him, leaving me in the lead!'

The European Championships, staged two months later at Haras du Pin, was a rather more serious affair in which Mark's first Union Jack saddle-cloth was to play its part. As Rock On moved through his dressage test, the saddle-cloth was seen to move back from underneath the saddle and then slowly down the horse's offside flank until it finally fluttered to the ground to be deftly retrieved by a French official. The British team and supporters (including Mark's parents) held their breath because Rock On's potential explosiveness was well known. But horse and rider continued the test unmoved and, in fact, were completely unaware of what had happened until it was all over. The lesson to Mark and others was well learned; ever since that day saddle-cloths have been securely attached to the numnah or saddle.

The cross-country fences had already given the British team enough cause for alarm. 'It was the biggest course I've ever ridden,' Mark said, with utter conviction.

'It was such a large course that initial concern turned to slightly amused amazement,' said Mark's father. 'As fence after fence was inspected, each appeared larger than the last – until, at the twenty-second, almost hysterical laughter broke out among the British team. Some of the other competitors, whose faces had been getting longer and longer, completely misinterpreted the rather strange British sense of humour and inquired as to whether they thought the course was rather too small.'

Both Mark and Princess Anne readily admit to the occasional jitters, especially during the interval between inspecting the cross-country fences for the first time and actually setting out to jump them. 'Usually, with nine fences out of ten,' said Mark, 'you have a plain and simple picture of something that's just there to be jumped, no matter how wide a ditch it might have or how big a drop. They don't really bother one in advance; you wouldn't be competing unless you had reasonable confidence in a horse's ability to jump that sort of fence.

'Where the bit of nerves enter into it, is when you have a problem fence and you can't work out in your own mind just how the horse is going to jump it. You can go over and over it in your head and still not get a clear picture of how to ride it.'

'My nerves,' said Princess Anne, 'are a mixture of total fright and the fear of total incompetence. Personally, I mind the simple straightforward fences more than I mind the complicated ones, for exactly the opposite reason. If they're simple and straightforward, the chances are that you lose concentration and make a nasty mess of it.'

'You always run that risk,' said Mark, 'but I think one of the lessons you learn, with experience, is *not* to lose concentration. At Haras du Pin I fell at just about the easiest fence on the cross-country course; it was literally just a hedge with a small drop. I went swanning into it, thinking: "This is an easy fence", and we turned upside down.'

Ironically, his mother (who hates watching him ride across country and normally doesn't) had decided to position herself at an easy fence; and the innocuous-looking hedge she chose was the very one at which Mark took a spine-chilling dive into bone-hard ground.

'I've never gone swanning into a fence like that again,' said Mark.

'*Never?*' asked Princess Anne. 'What about the time you were winning Liphook with Columbus?'

Mark grinned. 'That was *quite* different. I didn't lose my concentration at Liphook, I simply managed to turn the steering wheel
a split second too early so, instead of turning in mid-air, he turned
in front of the fence!'

The loss of concentration at Haras du Pin cost Mark third
place in the individual line-up. But, despite his fall and one refusal,
Rock On still had the fastest time across country – which (considering that the contestants included riders from Russia, East and
West Germany, Poland, France, Switzerland and Ireland) was
no mean achievement. The big cross-country course had decimated
the field by forty per cent, and of the twenty-two who did
complete the full test, only seven jumped clear rounds across
country.

But, for the British, it was another event to celebrate. Reunited with Cornishman V (whom Richard Meade had ridden
in Mexico) Mary Gordon-Watson won the individual title and
Richard Walker, who was that year's Badminton winner, finished
second. Richard, riding Pasha, was also on the winning team,
together with Derek Allhusen on Lochinvar, Pollyann Hely-
Hutchinson on Count Jasper and Ben Jones on The Poacher.

Mark Phillips had finished third best of the British contingent
and seventh individual over-all, so he had every reason to hope
for a place on the British team for the 1970 World Championships to be staged in Ireland the following year. But Rock On,
whose immensely promising career seemed doomed to frequent
interruption, went lame again shortly after Haras du Pin. His
tendency to jump everything as though it were the size of
Buckingham Palace put a great deal of extra pressure on his legs,
especially over drop fences.

There had been additional pressure in that Haras du Pin was
the second three-day event he had contested in the short space
of six weeks, for the selectors had insisted that he needed to prove
his fitness at the Punchestown three-day event in Ireland during
August if he were to be considered for the European Championships in September. It was to be almost two years before Rock
On was fit to compete again.

c

5 | Doublet, Purple Star and Chicago

From Princess Anne's viewpoint, the most important thing about 1969 was that it marked the beginning of her partnership with Doublet. By Doubtless II and out of Swate, who was one of Prince Philip's polo ponies, the Queen's handsome chestnut gelding had been bred for the polo field, whither he would certainly have been directed had he not grown to 16.2 hands. Instead he was sent to Alison Oliver with the hope that he would make a good event horse for the Princess.

It was Alison who rode Doublet in his first event. 'I can't remember why,' said Princess Anne, 'but it may have been because Alison thought he was too nappy. I know she took him to Hawley and, having jumped well into the water, he took one stride, landed on his knees and cut both of them. Yet, strangely enough, out of all the horses I've ridden he was the one who seemed to adore water.'

Oddly enough, that was also one of the first events in which Mark rode Great Ovation and he too has unpleasant memories of the Hawley water since he was eliminated there for three refusals. 'We took Great Ovation into it after the competition,' he said, 'and the following day we schooled him at the lake at Badminton, where he jumped into the water without any trouble!'

Alison confirmed that Doublet was by no means an easy ride when he first arrived at Warfield: 'He came to be a very reliable and consistent horse, but at that time he was quite nappy and rather highly-strung.' She had been an international rider herself before deciding that she would concentrate entirely on teaching, so it seemed sensible that she should introduce Doublet to the sport, while Princess Anne was enjoying one-day events with Purple Star and with another young horse, Royal Ocean, with whom she was also competing in novice classes.

Meanwhile, Doublet was fast becoming the great favourite in Alison Oliver's stable. 'Alison particularly likes certain horses,' said Princess Anne, 'and, for no particular reason, Doublet was one of them. So she applied even more tender, loving care.'

The horse had, in fact, become Alison's baby. 'I do tend to get very involved and possessive when I've had a horse and worked it,' she said. 'It's one of my dangers. I think it was probably quite difficult for Princess Anne to take over from me; I can really see it now, though I think it's something that she was aware of more than I was at the time.'

Alison had given up competitive riding herself because she was involved in training Princess Anne. 'She obviously had a lot of talent and was going to take eventing seriously. I then realized that I couldn't compete myself *and* train her *and* train other people. My competition horses were always very important to me so, when I rode other people's horses in competitions, I began to think of them as mine. I think this happened particularly with Doublet, although he was obviously for Princess Anne and there was no one else I would have wanted to ride him.'

Alison's possessiveness also underlines her virtues as a trainer; the work she puts into 'her' horses is very much a labour of love and it shows in the results she achieves. The difficulty is that she tends to be 'a little less sympathetic' when someone else takes the horse over and doesn't ride it quite as perfectly as she would like it to be ridden.

'I'm very aware of it now and so is Princess Anne,' said Alison. 'We joke about it now and so it doesn't occur in the same way. But I can see that there must have been times when it was a bit difficult for her with Doublet.'

Difficult or not, the Princess won her first novice one-day event with Doublet when she rode him at Osberton in the summer of 1969. Both he and Royal Ocean, who won at Windsor, were qualified for the inaugural Midland Bank Novice Championship to be incorporated in the Chatsworth Horse Trials that October – and both competed.

It was a tough course for novices and Royal Ocean went no further than the seventh cross-country fence where he was retired. But Doublet, lying equal first after the dressage, showed a definite touch of class by jumping a polished clear round across country. Then only a six-year-old, he had been ridden at a judicious pace and Princess Anne was perfectly content to finish sixth, twenty-one points behind Sarah Roger-Smith who won the Championship on Gambit.

Doublet was due to contest his first three-day event at Tidworth the following spring but a minor injury, while Princess Anne was touring Australia with the Queen and Prince Philip, thwarted this plan and Purple Star was entered in Doublet's place.

Alison Oliver was then expecting a baby and the Royal horses had therefore been moved to Lars Sederholm, for whom she had once worked. Lars runs a training establishment at Waterstock in Oxfordshire and it was one of his protégés, Richard Walker, who rode Doublet in the one-day event at Kinlet that year. It should have been a straightforward schooling exercise, a means to the end of getting the horse fit for Tidworth, instead of which Doublet fell at the Farmyard fence and a banged knee put him out of training.

Though Doublet was clearly her most promising horse, Princess Anne had great affection for Purple Star whom she was to ride at Tidworth in his place. 'He was such a character,' she said. 'Although he was never a particularly easy passage, he had all that was required – he really could jump and he hated touching anything, he was very fast across country and, because he was such a frightfully conceited little horse, he did a very flashy dressage whenever he bothered to pay attention. It was only in his later days that he began stopping whenever he thought he'd got himself seriously wrong – and he was undoubtedly the quickest stopper I've ever come across. I disappeared over his head so frequently that people used to say to Alison: "Why is she riding that dangerous horse when she keeps falling off it?" '

When she returned from Australia, the Princess had to do a

crash course to get fit for Tidworth. 'I remember driving up to Lars the day after I got back and riding three horses that afternoon; then I rode two more before breakfast the following morning.'

Lars was not, she decided, in the least bit impressed by Purple Star. It is therefore with a hint of relish that she describes the eye-opening training session during which her horse displayed one of his definite attributes: a blistering turn of foot. They had been cantering – Lars on Upper Strata and Princess Anne on Purple Star – when she was told to kick on and go a little faster. 'Purple left Upper Strata for dead,' she told me, 'and Lars was absolutely astonished.' (The Princess's later comment beside this description read: 'Slight exaggeration by proud owner!')

At the end of the dressage phase at Tidworth, Purple Star was well up with the leaders in fifth place, but two refusals across country dropped him to a lowly twenty-second as they went into the final show jumping. They were to finish even further down the line, for Purple Star put in one of his lightning refusals ('I think it was probably his quickest ever') and Princess Anne sailed on without him.

Pictures of her fall appeared in virtually every newspaper the following morning – 'but that wasn't so galling,' she said, 'as reading about the language I was *supposed* to have used.' This was quoted as: 'I saw bloody stars' – a perfectly reasonable remark under such circumstances but one which Princess Anne does *not* claim as her own: 'I didn't say anything, I was too surprised!'

The Princess's participation in three-day eventing undoubtedly contributed to the sport's rapid growth in Britain but she would clearly have been happier if she could have avoided the strains and stresses of all the attendant publicity. Her antipathy to photographers *en masse* is well known. 'It's not so much when I'm actually competing – that doesn't really bother me – it's the way they tend to keep getting in the way beforehand. Apart from anything else, one's always a bit wound up and worried before one starts. It's also that some appear so pleased when I fall off.'

The photographers are, of course, only there to do their job. But most of those who pursue her are news photographers and the most newsworthy picture they can get is one of Princess Anne turning upside-down with her horse. The Princess is much too intelligent to miss the sense of satisfaction that emanates from most of the photographers who happen to be beside a fence where she has a fall.

The sports pages tend to treat her more kindly, though in some cases only marginally so. The best example of newspaper attitudes came, in fact, from an equestrian correspondent, who was once told (albeit half-jokingly) that more space would be available for a three-day event report 'if someone lands on her regal bum'.

Such attitudes are hardly conducive to an easy relationship between the Princess and the Press. But she has learnt to recognize her allies. One man who photographed her icy dip into the Cattle Drinker at Rushall in 1975 showed genuine concern for her discomfort and she talked to him warmly, though through chattering teeth. 'He also refused to release his pictures to the newspapers,' said Princess Anne.

Tidworth in 1970 marked the virtual end of Purple Star's eventing career. 'Lars and I went back to school him over the cross-country fences he'd refused,' said the Princess, 'and I don't think Purple ever really forgave us. He hadn't stopped with any malice aforethought; he'd just treated the whole affair as fun – he'd never seen so many people and had thought they might like a better view of him! After that he completely went off the idea of eventing because he just didn't want to partake of the cross-country any more. Basically he was too clever by half and he didn't really see any sense in carrying on when he didn't actually enjoy it. But he was a charming horse, he taught me a fantastic amount and he never actually gave me a fall that had anything to do with his jumping a fence . . . it was only when he decided *not* to jump it!'

Purple Star therefore retired to the hunting field, which was much more to his taste and where he has been happy ever since.

The Princess herself also enjoys hunting, but contrary to a theory often propounded by the pundits of three-day eventing, neither she nor her husband believes that she suffered any disadvantage through not hunting as a child.

'I don't think hunting helps the jockey so much as the horse,' said Mark.

'I don't feel sorry that I hadn't hunted earlier,' said Princess Anne. 'I doubt if it would have made a great deal of difference.' She is not even convinced that hunting is beneficial for all prospective three-day event horses. 'I like to get to know them first and, if they're a bit nappy or a bit unsure of themselves, I like to hunt them. But if they're natural bold horses I don't honestly think it's worth it. Apart from anything else, the risks are far too great.'

While the Princess was in Australia Mark had been among the foot-sloggers for the 1970 Badminton Championship. There must have been moments when his trainer, Bertie Hill, wished that he had been following the event on foot as well – for, having survived the threat of incurring twenty penalties at the quarry, for what had initially been judged a technical refusal, he was eliminated for taking the wrong course in the show jumping. His mount, Chicago III, could otherwise have finished third; indeed, if he hadn't also lost time at the quarry on cross-country day, he might have won the Championship.

But eventing, as both Princess Anne and Mark Phillips would testify, tends to be full of 'might have' stories. Certainly fellow competitors reacted to the lapse with sympathy rather than criticism, for everyone knows all too well just how easy it is to make the odd fatal error.

It was the year in which the newly formed partnership of Richard Meade and Martin Whiteley's The Poacher triumphed at Badminton and, needless to say, both were included in the subsequent World Championship team. But the selectors also wanted Chicago III and, since Bertie Hill's professional status debarred him from contesting the world title, another rider had to be found. 'I was the lucky one who was chosen,' said Mark.

There was no hint of mock humility about the statement. Mark regards Chicago as one of the most brilliant horses he has ever encountered and, since his own international experience was then limited to one overseas contest, the invitation was naturally accepted as a great compliment. It was sad that the shambles of the

1970 World Championships didn't give them a better opportunity to display their combined skills.

'The course at Punchestown wasn't as big as the one at Haras du Pin,' said Mark. 'The trouble was that the fences were very narrow which meant that everyone had to jump them in the same place and, because it poured with rain all day, the ground became terribly slippery. Also the fences weren't made of substantial timber so they were continually breaking.'

To these problems were added the lack of provision for spectators. There was no special route prepared for them, so in order to walk the course, they had to clamber over the fences. The approaches and landings, which were already wet and muddy, therefore deteriorated into stretches of slush far more rapidly. A shortage of stewards to control the crowds meant that spectators were sometimes inside the penalty zone when a horse was actually jumping.

But the worst problem of all was fence 29, which combined a six-foot spread with a drop of at least five feet. Of the twenty-one horses who completed the course, no less than eight fell there and, when one considers that the chaff had been well and truly sorted from the wheat before that point, it would obviously have taken a quite appalling toll had it been one of the early fences. As it happened, the other nineteen horses who had set out that morning had fallen by the wayside before they reached fence 29 – and many of them were, perhaps, more than a little relieved.

Britain's team had been depleted when Benson, the mount of Stewart Stevens, failed to pass the veterinary inspection at the end of the roads and tracks and therefore couldn't attempt the cross-country. But Mary Gordon-Watson and Cornishman V had by then produced perhaps the most inspired performance of their distinguished career; intrepidly bold, they treated even the worst hazards like Pony Club fences and they finished with a clear round and a maximum bonus for time.

Benson's departure meant that both Mark Phillips on Chicago and Richard Meade on The Poacher would have to complete the course if Britain was to finish as a team and both of them set out full of gritty determination to do just that.

'Chicago,' according to Mark, 'went absolutely brilliantly until he had two falls at the 29th fence – neither of which was his fault. The spread was a wide parallel with a very big drop and the middle was filled with branches of fir that looked deceptively solid. It was just my luck that Chicago tried to bank it; he never saw the far rail, so he put his feet down in the middle and dropped straight through the fence. While I was on the ground some wretched person led him out through the side of the fence, instead of straight on under the far rail. This meant that he hadn't been through the flags so I had to go back and jump it again.

'There was a long delay while the fence was rebuilt and, by the time it was ready, the crowd had closed right in until they were actually inside the penalty zone. Chicago jumped the fence immaculately the second time, but he had to turn so sharply because of the crowds that he slipped up on the flat. We were inside the penalty zone, so that made another sixty penalties.'

Mark nevertheless finished the course and so did Richard Mcadc, who also had a fall at the infamous 29th. In fact, Richard's fall necessitated a visit to hospital where an injured shoulder had to be strapped up before he took part in the following day's show jumping. But the British team still won the world title – beating France, the only other nation to finish, by a massive margin of 436 points. Argentina, Ireland, Russia and West Germany had all been eliminated.

Individually, Mary Gordon-Watson and Cornishman V added the World Championship to the European title they had won in Haras du Pin the previous year. Richard Meade was second despite his fall and Mark Phillips, his admiration for Chicago greatly enhanced, finished in eleventh place.

6 | Success at Badminton

Mark was highly delighted by a plan, mooted a few months after the World Championships, which would have enabled him to continue riding Chicago. The horse was then up for sale and it was arranged that he would be bought by a British syndicate; Mark would thus be assured of a top-class mount and the horse's talents would not be lost to an overseas buyer.

The plan moved forward without a hitch until Chicago was inspected – and failed – by the British team vet, Peter Scott-Dunn. Subsequent events were to make that decision, reached through doubts about the horse's feet, look somewhat over-cautious. But by then Chicago had been sold to West Germany.

Mark, who had held high hopes concerning the Badminton Championships of 1971, was thus left (as he thought) with no chance at all. Chicago had been sold and Rock On was being prepared for the autumn; it was only to enable him at least to have a ride that Great Ovation, whom he owned jointly with his Aunt Flavia, was entered for Badminton.

Great Ovation had been bought on the recommendation of Bertie Hill, who knew the horse well since he had previously been sent to him to be broken. The 16.3½ hands gelding, by Three Cheers and out of Cyprus Valence, was not, however, an instant success. He had an infuriating and dangerous tendency to miss out the odd fence completely, giving Mark a number of painful falls. Mark had, in fact, missed the final trial at Eridge prior to the 1970 World Championships because he had hurt his back in a fall with Great Ovation.

Mark took him to Deurne, in Holland, just after the World

Championships – 'where he had yet another fall'. There had been talk of selling Great Ovation and, when Mark drove his father from the Dutch three-day event to the main-line station, Peter Phillips pressed him for a decision regarding the horse's future. 'We'll decide whether to sell him or keep him before I get on the train,' he said.

So Great Ovation's fate was eventually decided in a Dutch station buffet, over a cup of coffee. 'I'd like to give him one more go,' said Mark, 'so let's press on with him.' The pressing on was rewarded with victory in the Intermediate Section of the Rushall Horse Trials, followed by a third in the Advanced Class at Liphook, which was full of Badminton horses. These two outings prompted Mark to take the horse to Badminton – 'really just to give me a ride there'. Meanwhile Cornishman V was every tip-ster's favourite and Doublet was the horse who hogged the headlines, for he was to give Princess Anne her first taste of those awesome Gloucestershire fences.

Though she didn't know Mark well at the time, Princess Anne was to be made acutely aware of his presence among the field of forty-eight starters. She and Doublet were leading at the end of the first day of dressage – 'and right up until about four o'clock the following afternoon!' – until Mark went ahead with Great Ovation.

Mark was by then having second thoughts about tackling the cross-country course, primarily because the long dry spell had been succeeded by torrential rain and the going had rapidly deteriorated. Doubts concerning whether the horse would go on wet ground were added to doubts as to whether he was ready to tackle Badminton; Mark had therefore decided to pull out after the dressage.

'You can't pull out now,' said Bertie Hill, with whom Mark had, as usual, been staying during the final preparations for Bad-minton. 'You'll have to go on now you're leading in the dressage.' There was, no doubt, a certain amount of glee in Bertie's voice as he made his statement.

Great Ovation was the only horse to achieve a better score than Doublet; Princess Anne was therefore lying in second place as she set out to cover the fourteen miles that comprised the speed, endurance and cross-country phase.

'I didn't expect to get round,' she said, 'and Alison didn't expect me to get round either. She told me what to do if I had a fall, or two falls; she went into considerable detail about the sort of circumstances in which I ought to retire; but she didn't mention anything about weighing out at the finish.

'Parts of the course were just like a skating rink after all the rain, but Doublet went really well. The only place I had any trouble was at the Baby Elephant Trap; he was looking at the crowds and he almost missed it out. I gave him a couple up – in fact it was the only time in my life that I ever hit him – and he went very, very well after that.

'My main problem was that I almost strangled myself! My stock wasn't quite tight enough and it had slipped down so that the knot caught me right in the base of the throat . . . a quite unnecessary additional hazard! I literally had to ride with my head down between fences and then take a deep breath before looking up. I was absolutely puce in the face by the time I finished.'

But finish she did and Alison, who vehemently denies that she hadn't expected her pupil to make it, was there at the box to greet her. With a third of the field gone, Princess Anne was in the lead for the Badminton Championship. Great Ovation was, however, still to come.

The eight-year-old's jumping was greatly improved but he was never a particular pleasure to ride across country, for the simple reason that he had to be pushed virtually every yard of the way. Whereas Princess Anne said she was always 'gasping' at the end of the cross-country phase of a three-day event, Mark said he was 'only gasping after riding Great Ovation'.

So it was without the enthusiasm which might have been anticipated by those who studied only the bare results that Mark described the horse's performance at Badminton: 'He jumped a reasonable round but there was nothing very brilliant about it.'

'Actually, he happened to be a lot faster than most of the others,' said Princess Anne a trifle caustically.

'I was helped there,' said Mark. 'I was stopped half-way round because another horse had fallen at the Normandy Bank. I must have had a ten to fifteen minute break so, although I really hadn't gone very fast to begin with, I pushed on a bit, knowing that the horse was fresh again after his rest and that there wasn't that much further to go.'

Well, everyone needs a touch of luck to win a three-day event and no one would have disputed Mark's right to hold the lead at the end of the day. Great Ovation was, in fact, almost twenty points ahead, followed by Mary Gordon-Watson on Cornishman V and Richard Walker on Upper Strata, both of whom had moved narrowly ahead of Princess Anne with Doublet.

During the time that Great Ovation might have been sold a Dutchman and an American had been to see him at Great Somerford. Mark's father met the Dutchman at the veterinary inspection, on the morning after the cross-country phase, and was asked whether the horse was still for sale.

'I don't know,' said Peter Phillips, 'but I very much doubt it.'

'If he were for sale,' asked the Dutchman, 'what sort of price would you be asking?'

'If he were for sale (and I don't think he is) the price would be £10000.'

'That's much more than we were talking about before.'

'I know it's more,' said Peter Phillips, 'but circumstances have rather changed.'

The changed circumstances meant that Great Ovation was last into the arena that afternoon for the final show jumping phase, run, as is now the usual practice, in the reverse order of merit. Before he appeared, Princess Anne had slipped back by one place.

'The Olivers had given me two different versions about how to jump the water and I didn't get either of them right! Doublet had never seen a water jump in a show jumping arena before (neither had I) and it took him completely by surprise. I hadn't got in quite close enough and, as he took off, I think he imagined that he was supposed to jump into the water and couldn't understand why I was going quite so fast. The expression on his face in the photographs showed total astonishment. Anyway, I was thrilled; we hadn't actually knocked any fences down and I felt it was a tremendous achievement to finish fifth. In fact, I was a bit peeved when everyone started carping about Doublet jumping into the bottom of the water.'

Debbie West wasn't carping, for Doublet's lapse and another by Upper Strata had pushed her up to third place on Baccarat. But there was no catching Great Ovation. A single mistake by Cornishman V had given Mark two fences in hand, but he didn't need either of them for the horse jumped a good clear round. Since the selectors, quite rightly, base most of their decisions on the results of Badminton, Mark was assured of a place on the team for that year's European Championship.

It was much more intriguing to speculate on the chances of Princess Anne's being chosen to ride for Britain. Far from supposing that her Royal birth would give her an advantage, there were many of us who wondered whether the selectors would be reluctant to submit a member of the Royal Family to the risk of injury. But, as has happened throughout the Princess's eventing career, the selectors refused to yield to either consideration; they treated her as a normal sportswoman and simply went by the formbook.

Thus, Princess Anne and Doublet were short-listed to compete as individuals. The only concession made to the Royal title was in the wording of the official announcement, which seemed aimed at deflecting a flood of queries from the uninformed by stating:

'The selectors were greatly impressed by Princess Anne's performance on Doublet at Badminton. However, since this was the first international competition for both of them, and in view of the very large number of experienced combinations available, it was not thought advisable to include Her Royal Highness on the short-list of eight from which the team will be chosen. But Great Britain will be allowed to enter approximately twelve individuals, in addition to the team, as the host nation. Princess Anne is being invited to fill one of these vacancies.'

7 | A European title

'Then I went to Canada in May, and in the middle of July, I was in hospital.' This was the start of Princess Anne's account of the events between Badminton at the end of April and the European Championships at Burghley in early September – and it sounded as deceptively simple as the beginning of a Hemingway novel.

The Canadian tour had been pre-planned and pre-announced, it was all part of the accepted pattern; but the Princess's admission to hospital for an operation was outside the bounds of normality and it was therefore the event which made banner headlines. But, among the followers of three-day eventing, it was not so much a sensational fact as a cause for speculation: would she be out and ready and fit in time for the final trial at Eridge to be held six weeks later?

Most people thought not. Alison Oliver didn't believe there was any possibility that her Royal pupil could be fit in time. 'Until, that is, I went to see her in hospital and realized that she was utterly determined to go ahead. I think it was then that I really appreciated the extent of her dedication and knew that she was made of the right stuff.'

'I had a little trouble in hospital,' said Princess Anne, 'because I couldn't persuade any of the doctors to believe that I really did intend to try for Eridge and Burghley. I'd say: "Aren't there such people as physiotherapists?" And they'd say: "Yes, of course, but let's worry about that a little later."'

'When I came out, I went to see two people who had put my family together after various illnesses. One of them was a physio-therapist and when she heard that I'd been given no "physio" treatment at all in hospital, she said: "*What?* They do it for every-one else!" She then gave me a book of exercises and, for the only time in my life, I actually did them.

'Later I went to Balmoral for about a week and did as much walking as I could up and down hills. Then I had a week on the yacht, during which I tried to take as much reasonable exercise as possible. When I got back, about four days before the final trial at Eridge, I was saying to myself: "Well, it feels all right at the moment but, if I do get a twinge, I won't bother to go on." Doublet led after the dressage at Eridge, but he was a bit bold going through that funny water jump and he couldn't get out over the rail. And then I fell off.'

'You would have won otherwise,' said Mark.

'Of course,' said Princess Anne. '*The old story*. I would have won if the horse hadn't stopped and I hadn't fallen off. Actually, in spite of that and for the first time in history, I had the equal fastest time of the day – and nobody was more surprised than I was. I know I made a bit of a mess of the cross-country but I was still thrilled, because the horse had gone very well and I wasn't feeling any the worse for wear. So then I thought it would probably be all right for Burghley.'

Mark Phillips had meanwhile won the advanced class of the Eridge Horse Trials on Great Ovation, thereby adding what little confirmation was needed to the inevitability of his selection for the British team. His own moment of near-disaster was, however, still to come for on the journey from Eridge to the training venue at Ascot, Great Ovation, somehow lost his feet in the trailer. He was travelling with Rock On, who was just back in harness and had finished seventh at Eridge, and between them the two horses made a formidable commotion. Mark, alone at the steering wheel, listened to it in horror.

'I had to pull up in the middle of East Grinstead,' he said. 'When I let the ramp down, Rock On came charging out and he disappeared down East Grinstead High Street, followed by a policeman. The partition had been kicked into matchwood by that stage and Great Ovation was still on the floor. When I eventually managed to get him back on his feet, I discovered that he had taken all the skin off one hip. But fortunately he was otherwise unharmed – and Rock On, who was finally caught in a pub car park, was all right as well.'

The period of collective training was supposed to be exclusively for the four riders who had been chosen for the team, and the two reserves. But Princess Anne, although she didn't come into this category, did most of her training with them, 'because I was living next-door, so to speak'. Windsor Castle is not 'next door' to Ribblesdale Park in the suburban sense of the term but, since the team were using Windsor Great Park for their training, they were (so to speak) sharing the same back garden.

When Bill Thompson's European Championship course was finally unveiled, it looked eminently fair, beautifully constructed and more than a little testing. 'I can remember thinking that I'd never in my life seen anything as big,' said Princess Anne, with feeling.

'It wasn't as big as Badminton,' Mark told her, matter-of-factly.

'Well *you* may not have thought so. But there were those three spread fences after the coffin and they were certainly wider than anything I'd seen before. They worried me because I'd never thought that Doublet was particularly good at spreads, and I didn't think he'd enjoy the hard going very much either.'

Alison Oliver, who had put in much dedicated background work in order to have the horse fit to run for his life on cross-country day, mentioned the problem imposed by the spread fences more specifically. 'Doublet was marvellous in many ways; he was very agile and clever; he was honest and bold. But he hadn't the limitless scope of Goodwill or Columbus who, if they meet a spread from a long way off, can throw an enormous leap. Therefore it demanded more accurate riding and Princess Anne was aware that she couldn't afford to meet the spreads too far out.' Alison was, however, conscious of a 'certain excitement' as she walked the course with her pupil: 'Here was the challenge and one thought that it might just work out right.'

The preceding dressage was expected to give the Princess a good start, for Doublet had already shown that he had an out-

D

standing aptitude for this particular phase. 'In the end, you could more or less have shoved him in a big arena,' said Princess Anne, 'and he would have done a good test almost on his own.' This was obviously an over-simplification, since the Princess was rather more than a passenger, but she probably was flattered by the horse in that she didn't have to work as hard before and during the dressage as most other riders.

As Mark pointed out: 'There aren't that many Doublets around and most good tests don't just happen. To do a really good test, I think you have to start with a horse that has a natural cadence and a natural presence; then it's just a matter of temperament. But it can be very hard work. Great Ovation was leading in the dressage at Badminton that year, but I'd gone in with my shirt literally sticking to me from all the exertion beforehand. It was a good deal wetter when I came out!'

Doublet possessed the cadence and the presence and the temperament. He also had that element of showmanship that belongs to all the truly great horses: he loved an audience. Princess Anne recalled one occasion at Badminton, when they were waiting in the cold and the drizzle, and Doublet seemed thoroughly disenchanted with the whole event. But, as soon as he walked into the arena and surveyed the crowds and the television cameras, he was in his element.

He was in his element, too, at Burghley, where enormous crowds had gathered to watch the European Championships in general and the Princess in particular. Unlike most horses who tend to be distracted or (worse still) intoxicated by large crowds, Doublet had a remarkable ability to concentrate on the job in hand. He produced a lovely rhythmic and accurate test and finished the first phase in the lead. This was something of a revelation to the overseas competitors who had arrived from Italy, France, Russia, Switzerland, Ireland and Holland (as full teams) and from West Germany and Sweden (as individuals). They had been intrigued by the Princess's Royal title but they hadn't even thought of rating her as a serious competitor.

Most people probably weren't convinced even then for, while dressage could be considered a suitable sport for princesses, the speed, endurance and cross-country test certainly could not. It covered more than seventeen miles and culminated in a four-and-three-quarter-mile cross-country section over thirty-three big solid fences. Everybody still expected that cross-country day would change the top placings, including Princess Anne herself.

'I set off thinking I might just about get round,' she said. 'Then, after all the worries about Doublet not liking the hard ground, I realized that he was thoroughly enjoying himself; he thought it was lovely from the word go. I actually began rather to enjoy it myself, once I'd jumped those three big fences and survived the Trout Hatchery. I tried – how I tried! – to trot into the Trout Hatchery, but Doublet wouldn't have it. He then created so much spray cantering through the water that he got one leg completely left behind and had nothing to push off with when he reached the bank on the other side.'

That one near-squeak was to be much analysed in Press reports and in television action replays. Some of them, perhaps, were a bit too lyrical, for the Princess simply did what any good rider would do; she gave her horse every assistance to get himself out of trouble by taking her weight off the saddle and giving him plenty of rein. I have seen Princess Anne make one or two genuinely spectacular recoveries from heart-in-the-mouth situations, but that wasn't one of them.

Once he had heaved himself out of the water, Doublet recaptured his rhythmic, ground-eating stride. Most riders exuded an air of grim purpose; Princess Anne made it look like a carefree holiday spin. Her round on Doublet was to leave a lasting impression of lightness and speed and agility. It was also to leave the Russian assistant-director of sports medicine, who had travelled with the Soviet team, in a state of worried perplexity. Those members of his all-male team who had succeeded in completing the course looked thoroughly exhausted, whereas Princess Anne, and most of the other British girls, appeared to take it all in their stride. Like Victorian ladies, they were not sweating or perspiring, but merely glowing.

As she finished the Princess hoped, rather than knew, that her time would prove a fast one. 'I was dead ignorant about that sort of thing. I just knew that the horse had gone very well and that we'd been a bit faster than we were at Badminton. But I certainly didn't expect to be the second fastest.' The only rider to achieve a better time was Stewart Stevens, another British individual, but he had incurred a hefty deficit in the dressage arena with Classic Chips and was still more than forty points behind, in fourth place.

News of Doublet's score percolated rapidly. 'It was very boring for the rest of us,' Mark told his wife, 'because, no matter how well any of us had gone, we couldn't have beaten you.' In fact, Mark was to make a decision for which he has probably been kicking himself ever since. At the penultimate fence, he aimed Great Ovation at a V-shaped corner, which could be taken as one jump, rather than settle for the slower but safer route over the two separate arms of the obstacle. Great Ovation thus marred an otherwise clear round with a run-out that cost him twenty penalties and second place.

At the end of cross-country day, Princess Anne held a lead of 27.8 points. It seemed substantial enough to the rest of us, but the Princess with the prize so nearly in her grasp and with all the attendant pressures that that implies, simply felt 'worried sick' about the show jumping. She was, she readily admits, far more nervous before the final phase than at any other stage of the competition. Even though a single mistake by Debbie West on Baccarat had increased her lead by another ten points, she was taking nothing for granted.

'Doublet was never particularly good at show jumping,' she said, 'and I was determined not to take chances with the first few fences, as I had done in other events. People said he jumped pawkily, which indeed he did, but that was because I'd decided that he took time to warm up and that there was no point in asking him to crack on until he was ready. When he cleared the third last, which a good many horses had down, I remember thinking that if we splashed into the water and crashed through the last (as long as we didn't fall) we would still win the Championship.' As it transpired she won with a clear round and later received the Raleigh Trophy from her delighted mother.

The Princess's victory naturally overshadowed the success of the British team, who beat Russia by a thumping great margin of 422.2 points. The four team members finished in close proximity in the individual placings: Debbie West was second on Baccarat, Mary Gordon-Watson fourth on Cornishman V, Richard Meade fifth on The Poacher and Mark Phillips sixth on Great Ovation, despite his débâcle at the penultimate cross-country fence.

'Afterwards,' said Princess Anne, 'everybody kept telling me that it was, of course, the team success that really mattered!'

Be that as it may, it was the Princess's victory that gave three-day eventing a far more prominent place on the sporting map of Britain. Those of us who write for newspapers had a special cause for gratification; the difference between the various equestrian disciplines was now clearly established and sub-editors no longer wrote 'show jumping' at the top of our three-day event reports.

That year, the Princess scooped all the 'personality' prizes. She won the Sportswriters' Award, was named the *Daily Express* Sportswoman of the Year and the BBC Television Sports Personality of the Year. Then there was an entertaining, totally irrelevant shindy – for which Harvey Smith, with his special flair for attracting maximum publicity from minor statements, was once again responsible.

'In her own class she is the best there is,' he said, 'but that is nowhere near Olympic standards. I certainly wouldn't like to see them pick her for the Olympics, despite the way the Press is clamouring for it.' It could have been argued that to be 'the best there is' in a sport which happens to be included in the Olympic Games might actually justify selection, but to produce logical argument would have been to miss all the fun. Instead there were urgent phone calls to the gentlemen of three-day eventing, who made gallant statements on Princess Anne's behalf.

More serious, in some eyes, was the fact that Harvey (not content with knocking the Princess) had the unforgivable effrontery to knock the sport as well. He claimed, in a quite remarkable display of *lèse-majesté*, that a fourth-rate professional show jumper entering Princess Anne's sport 'would clear the deck of every prize, in every event, every time'. Richard Meade challenged him to put his money where his mouth was, so to speak, by riding for a wager at Badminton. The challenge wasn't publicly declined but, since all good things must come to an end, the whole thing had died a natural death by the time the 1972 Badminton came around.

By then we were all involved in the feverish business of predicting who might be chosen for the Olympics. The Princess obviously came into the reckoning, but, though some writers awarded her a place on the team without further ado, most of us maintained that she would have to back up her European title with a good performance at Badminton.

It was not then generally known that Doublet had developed leg trouble at Burghley, which wasn't considered serious at the time. Princess Anne believes that the problem stemmed from the efforts to extricate himself from the Trout Hatchery ('I think he must have trodden on himself getting out') but there was still every reason to hope that he would be fit in time for Badminton. His preparations were almost complete when Alison decided to give him a thorough work-out, after which it was decided that the sprained tendon wouldn't stand Badminton or the Olympics. So the horse was withdrawn from Badminton less than a week before the competition was due to start and he was turned away for the year.

'Almost my most vivid impression of that time,' said Princess Anne, 'was Doublet's reaction to being roughed off. He seemed thoroughly depressed and looked at one with eyes that said: "What have I done wrong?" '

8 | The Munich Olympics

Rock On, whom Mark had always regarded as a better horse than Great Ovation, was also withdrawn from Badminton. He had been with the British team that travelled to the 'Mini-Munich' three-day event the previous autumn when, with just one fence left to jump in the final show jumping phase, he had looked certain to achieve a convincing victory. Mark himself had already counted his chickens and, knowing that the prize was his whether he hit or cleared the last, made the fatal mistake of relaxing a second too soon. Rock On, allowed to stride on unchecked, took off disastrously early, landed into a mass of flying poles and turned upside down. The fall cost 41.25 penalties and dropped him to fifth place, leaving another British rider, Lorna Sutherland on Peer Gynt, as the winner.

Much worse was to follow for Rock On, having suffered a recurrence of his leg trouble, underwent a tendon operation in 1972 and died shortly afterwards. He had come out of the anaesthetic and was eating his mash, in apparent unconcern, when he suddenly dropped dead.

'We all felt terrible,' said Mark's mother, who had a special soft spot for the brave and talented horse whom she had nicknamed Joe ('because he was so sloppy in the stable'). All the Phillipses' horses tend to be referred to by sobriquets and it takes the newcomer some time to realize that Cheers is, in fact, Great Ovation, Percy is Persian Holiday and so on. Princess Anne appears to have caught the habit for she now refers to her novice Mardi Gras by the singularly unprepossessing name of Grot.

A post mortem was to reveal that Rock On's death was unconnected with his operation, which relieved the Phillips family without mitigating their sense of loss. A small nodule had detached itself from inside the aorta and several more were found to be present; no one knows how they got there, but each one was potentially lethal. Had he contested another three-day event, he might well have dropped dead during the competition.

For Mark, with that special sense of attachment which all riders feel for their first truly great horse, it was a grievous personal loss as well as a blow to his sporting ambitions. But he still had Great Ovation to ride at Badminton and, though he had to push him on more visibly across country than during the previous year, he won the great classic for the second successive time.

He won it, in fact, in one of the most spectacular finales ever seen at Badminton, for Richard Meade, a decimal point ahead on Laurieston when the show jumping phase began, jumped an over-deliberate clear round and collected 1.25 time penalties. Strangely enough, though many people in the stands and all those watching their television sets were acutely aware that Laurieston might have been over the time allowed, the two principals were totally oblivious of the impending announcement. Mark, who had been standing beside Laurieston's owner, Major Derek Allhusen, while Richard was jumping, simply registered that there were no jumping penalties; he turned and congratulated his companion with one of those warm, flashing smiles that melted so many female hearts on the day of the Royal Wedding. Meanwhile Richard rode out of the arena wearing that special look of decency and modesty with which so many English sportsmen mask their jubilation. And then the bombshell dropped: no jumping penalties for Laurieston, but 1.25 time penalties. Mark and Great Ovation had won.

Thinking back to the previous day, Mark felt that there was some sort of justice about the final result. His stop-watch had failed him on the steeplechase course, and, as a result, he had incurred 8.8 unnecessary penalties. But, although everyone loves to see their name as many times as possible on Badminton's roll of honour, the event is more of a stepping-stone during the Olympic year than an end in itself; for both riders the knowledge that they had earned a place on the Olympic team was more

Princess Anne on Doublet – 'out of all the horses I've ridden he was the one who seemed to adore water'.

LEFT AND BELOW: Great Ovation in the show jumping at Burghley and receiving the champion's rosette from the Queen at Badminton. There had been talk of selling the horse in 1970 until Mark said: 'I'd like to give him one more go.'

OPPOSITE PAGE: Princess Anne, photographed with Peter Dimmock (*left*) and Henry Cooper, is the 1971 BBC Television Sports Personality of the Year.

Below: Preparations for the 1972 Olympics. Mark, seen with Bridget Parker on Cornish Gold and Richard Meade on Laurieston, was worried about Great Ovation – 'There wasn't anything I could really put my finger on; I just knew that he wasn't quite right.'

Goodwill in the dressage arena and the show jumping ring. 'He used to argue about stopping,' said Princess Anne, 'which he still does – but for a much shorter space of time.'

Trainers and riders. Left to
right: Alison Oliver,
Mark Phillips, Princess Anne,
Bertie Hill, and Sheila Willcox.

Left: Mark and Brazil about to
dive into the Badminton lake.

OPPOSITE PAGE: Rushall,
1975. Princess Anne and Mardi
Gras take an icy dip in the
Cattle Drinker.

Since their marriage they have complemented each other. 'I think my dressage has improved no end,' said Mark, 'and I think Princess Anne's cross-country has also improved.'

important than whether they stood first or second in the final line-up.

Earlier, Doublet's withdrawal from the event had led to brief speculation as to whether Princess Anne would accept the Badminton Committee's invitation to ride the Queen's seven-year-old Columbus there instead. The horse was short of experience rather than fitness, for he had been working with Doublet and was physically quite ready to tackle a three-day event. The idea was given serious consideration and urgent discussion took place at Alison Oliver's home but it was finally (and most would say wisely) rejected.

The Princess has met with no family objections to her participation in three-day eventing at any level – 'except when they were under the misguided impression that Columbus was a dangerous horse'. So, no doubt, there was family relief when she plumped for the nice straightforward fences at Tidworth a little later, rather than the ogres of Badminton, for her first three-day event with Columbus. Even then they may have retained several misgivings.

Columbus, a 17 hands grey gelding by Colonist II and out of Princess Alexandra's hunter mare Trim Ann, had always been bold and headstrong and afraid of nothing. 'It was the fields rather than the fences that got the better of me at Tidworth,' said Princess Anne. 'He never took off when approaching a fence; it was in turning corners and in steadying between fences that the problems arose. There was a long gallop towards trees near the end of the course and I realized that we were never going to get through them in one piece at the speed we were going, so I had to circle him to slow him down. But he never came near to giving me a fall any time I rode him.' Columbus's braking and steering problems also resulted in refusals at the two fences which comprised the Cross Belt Corner at Tidworth and he finished well down in the placings.

Meanwhile, the horses on the Olympic short-list were enjoying a well-earned rest after their efforts at Badminton. Some may have been pleased, or puzzled, by a certain degree of extra concern for their welfare, but they still grazed their way peacefully through a month or two of late spring and early summer. Then they were meticulously prepared for the final trial at Eridge, for which they were to be joined by the United States Olympic team in its full, and ominous, strength.

As it transpired, it proved to be a hazardous final trial for both the British and the Americans. Cross-country day had started sunnily enough to snare many of those bound for Eridge into dressing for a hot, dry day. But rain then fell with relentless ferocity from late morning onwards, transforming what had been excellent going into slimy, treacherous sludge. To make matters worse, the stream into which horses jumped at fence 23 had become almost unnegotiable. The landing, hidden underwater, must have been murderously uneven, for more than half of those who jumped into it failed to stay on their feet. Great Ovation and Lauriston fell there, so did two of the American horses. It was clearly a dangerous jump and later riders were directed to by-pass it.

So the final outing for the British Olympic team can scarcely be said to have gone according to plan, but the selectors were undismayed. After all, the horses that fell were unhurt; they had gone on to complete the course and, like the rest of the team, they looked wonderfully fit and well. It was Great Ovation who was dismayed by the day's proceedings.

'He hated the slippery going,' said Mark, 'and I think the fall at the water was really the final straw.' The extent of Great Ovation's disenchantment with cross-country courses was not then apparent but Mark was full of niggling doubts throughout an anxious week in Munich, during which the team was preparing to play its part on the Olympic stage. 'There wasn't anything I could really put my finger on; I simply knew that he wasn't quite right.'

Laurieston, meanwhile, was back to his chirpy self; the other two horses nominated for the team – Mary Gordon-Watson's Cornishman V and Debbie West's Baccarat – were working well and happily. But for poor Debbie the end was to come prematurely, on the day before the Olympic three-day event began, when Baccarat went lame and Cornish Gold, ridden by Bridget Parker, had to be brought in to fill his place.

Great Ovation was to produce the best dressage score of the British team, but Mark's worries lingered on. As he set out on the speed, endurance and cross-country journey, he was still painfully aware that his dual Badminton winner was not yet back to his best form. He received positive and unwelcome proof when the horse had two falls and two refusals across country. The first fall, at fence 4, was out of character for Great Ovation, since he had stood right off at a wide spread. While Mark was remounting one rein became looped over the horse's nose, which naturally affected his steering, but he nevertheless continued on to the Sunken Road, at fence 19, where the misplaced rein caused a technical refusal.

Mark had been third to go for the British team, but he hadn't managed to emulate the two fine performances of Mary Gordon-Watson and Bridget Parker (both of whom had just one refusal at the bogey 23rd fence) and put Britain in the lead. It was left to Richard Meade to wipe away the handicap of those 160 jumping penalties and he did so in magnificent style on Laurieston, earning himself an individual gold medal in the process.

Great Ovation, though virtually certain to have the discard score, did boost morale on the final day when he jumped a good clear round in the show jumping. Mark then watched his team-mates clinch the gold medal and it was, he says, one of the most thrilling moments of his life.

It was a great thrill too for Princess Anne, who followed the competition with intense interest and joined in the euphoric celebrations. Then she returned home to continue her training sessions on Columbus, whom she was to ride at Burghley later that month. The preparatory work did not, however, bear much fruit. Columbus was galloping like a runaway train on the steeplechase course and the Princess decided that (as soon as she could actually manage to stop him) she would call it a day and retire.

'We'd found the brakes to stop him,' she said, referring to the gag snaffle Columbus was due to wear on the cross-country, 'but we foolishly didn't use it on the steeplechase. If I'd been a bit braver or a bit stronger, I would probably have kept going; also if people hadn't kept saying: "Don't worry if you have any problems, you just retire." It was probably right to stop when I did, but I must admit that I was a bit annoyed with myself afterwards.'

So the Raleigh Trophy, which the Princess had collected the previous year when winning the European Championship on Doublet, found a new home. It went to Janet Hodgson and her big bold Irish hunter, Larkspur.

Meanwhile the future of Columbus had to be resolved. He was clearly too strong for feminine muscles, so a male jockey would have to be found for him if he were to continue in eventing the following year. Princess Anne then thought of Mark Phillips.

'I didn't really know him at the time, but I thought he was the most sympathetic of the good men I'd ever seen riding. He's very, very strong (horses rarely stop with him and, if they do, they rather wish they hadn't) but he's also very sympathetic to different types of horses which, I think, is rare in men. I said to Alison at Burghley that I thought, with Mother's approval, he would be the person to ask to ride Columbus.'

So, in the autumn of 1972, Mark was invited to weld a new partnership with the Queen's big, rangy, impetuous and talented horse. It seemed conceivable that it might lead him to another Badminton Championship, but no one (least of all those closely involved) realized that it would also lead him to a Royal Wedding.

9 | Columbus and Goodwill

The gossip columnists, flourishing on the 'who's been seen with whom' syndrome, scented romance as soon as the Princess and Mark began training for the 1973 Badminton Championship. There was not, however, any particular significance in the fact that they trained together; both were riding three-day event horses owned by the Queen and, as had happened since they embarked on the sport, both horses were in Alison Oliver's care.

But some of the training sessions, which should have been concentrated and private, ended up as a game of evading the photographers who were lurking in the bushes. And when the Princess and Mark made their first competitive appearance of the year – at the Amberley Horse Show in Cirencester Park – the venue looked more like a grand reunion of Press photographers than a sporting occasion.

Despite the distractions, the Princess won a novice dressage class on Flame Gun and a novice section of the one-day event on Mark's Persian Holiday. She had, in the process, survived one king-sized blunder made by Persian Holiday at the twelfth fence, appropriately enough called Anne's Maze. It was to be recorded for posterity by a solid battery of photographers, who captured the moment when Princess Anne, having let go of the reins, looked as though she were trying to fly away from a horse that was about to make a large dent in the ground. A fall seemed inevitable but, in a balancing act that would have impressed Mr Bertram Mills, Persian Holiday kept his feet while the Princess regained her seat and her reins and galloped away.

'I'm a pessimist,' she said. 'If the horse touches anything I invariably think that I'm bound to fall over, so I take very quick avoiding action.'

A natural, inborn sense of balance is, of course, essential for any rider who aspires to reach the top of the ladder in three-day eventing. As Mark pointed out: 'If you were to look back through the photographs of most top riders, you would find plenty that showed them at various ends of buckles and hanging on by various fingernails. You can only go so far by learning to push buttons. But to get to the top and stay there I think you must have natural ability, including natural balance.'

It was during that spring that Mark's own fingernails weren't much use to him, for the simple reason that his horses weren't just making blunders, they were actually falling. Somerset Morn came down with him at Amberley; Columbus hit the deck (for the second time that season) at Rushall the following week. And he hit it with sickening force.

When walking the course, Mark had decided to jump the V-shaped 'Caroline's Elbow' in the corner as one jump, rather than in the centre as two. But a bad ride there with Great Ovation, who was to attempt a Badminton hat-trick two weeks later, prompted him to try different tactics with Columbus. The horse, unfortunately, knew the fence, for he had jumped it (at the corner) the previous year with Princess Anne. Aimed at the centre, he tried to jump both parts in one, from a totally impossible angle, and he paid the inevitable and painful penalty. Mark was concussed and lost the sight of his right eye for twenty-four hours; when he emerged from the St John's Ambulance later that day he looked like the shattered hero of a British war film. It was clearly not a role that he wished to play with either Great Ovation or Columbus at Badminton.

Meanwhile Princess Anne was enjoying a build-up to Badminton that comfortingly coincided with the pre-arranged plan. She was to ride the Queen's eight-year-old Goodwill, bought from Harvey Smith's former partner Trevor Banks the previous year on the advice of Alison Oliver.

'Alison had one of her rare holidays,' said the Princess, 'and she went out to the Rome Show with Alan' (Alison's show jumping husband). 'Trevor Banks was also there, and when he said: "I've got just the horse for Princess Anne," she immediately pricked up her ears. She's always been very good at weeding out the possibles from the impossibles.'

So Goodwill, a 16.2 hands brown gelding by Evening Trial, was loaded on to the box that was to bring the Smith–Banks show jumpers to the Royal Windsor Horse Show in May 1972. He was taken to Alison's nearby establishment at Warfield, where Princess Anne tried him out.

They began in the school ('where I got carted at the trot,' said the Princess), and then they tried the show jumps; since the horse had previously reached international level when jumped by Alison Dawes, most people would have expected him to pop over a smallish course with the utmost nonchalance.

But Alison, quite rightly as it transpired, didn't expect anything at all. 'I tend to get a horse and then find out what it's like, without expecting anything in advance. If you have a preconceived idea it's nearly always proved wrong.'

It would certainly have been proved wrong by Goodwill. 'There was a lane of about four fences,' said Princess Anne, 'and once I'd turned into them I had no further effect on the proceedings. We then took him up to the novice cross-country fences on Smith's Lawn and he was a completely different horse. He didn't pull my arms out; he seemed perfectly relaxed and he just pottered over the cross-country fences as though it was something he really enjoyed. He had reached Grade A show jumping exceptionally quickly as a young horse and I think it worried him; he seemed to associate show jumps with pressure. But the cross-country really impressed us – and he hadn't seen a cross-country fence since he was hunted as a four-year-old.

'In every other respect he was a dead loss when we first got him. He was a completely different shape and much too strong for himself; it was as though he was trying to control all that energy and didn't know how to. The first time we asked him to gallop he was completely at sea and his legs were all over the place; he used to gallop with his nose on the ground, which meant one got very tired from having to try to haul his head up every time he approached a fence. He also used to argue about stopping, which he still does – but for a much shorter space of time.'

Goodwill, schooled by Princess Anne under Alison Oliver's instruction, was a much improved horse by the time he was being prepared for Badminton. He had also displayed his jumping talent in a somewhat original way. 'In one of his first novice events,' said the Princess, 'he ran out at a corner and jumped the fence beyond it; he was too quick for words. Of course, I instantly got myself eliminated without even trying.'

Contestants for the 1973 Badminton Championship were united in their total abhorrence of the new dressage test, being tried out for the first time at an international three-day event. Even Mark, who was leading on Great Ovation at the end of that phase, came out strongly against the innovation. Princess Anne was rather more vehement in her objections, because 'it set Goodwill's dressage back by about a year. Those stupid flying changes got him into the most terrible state; he really wasn't ready to tackle that level of dressage and I think he associated the flying changes with his show jumping days.' There might well have been a riot had the test, with all its fussy transitions so totally unsuited to bold cross-country horses, been retained for another year; but it was wisely thrown out like a rotten egg.

By cross-country day the 1973 Badminton story, with all its romantic sub-plots, had moved towards Mark's attempt to win the great classic for the third successive year with Great Ovation. The morning had seemed like a commercial for the latest thrilling instalment of a popular serial: 'Can a new record be achieved today? Can Great Ovation become the first horse to win Badminton three times?' The afternoon brought sad anti-climax with the news that Great Ovation had gone lame on the roads and tracks, and had been withdrawn.

It was the second disappointment of the day for Mark, since Columbus had kept his dispiriting record for the spring season intact by falling yet again – and not once, but twice. Ironically enough, it was the gag snaffle (which Princess Anne regretted not using on the steeplechase course at Burghley) that put him on the floor at Badminton. The Princess had felt she needed the gag ('for my own self-confidence') but had rarely used it. It was sufficient to know that she could stop should the need arise; meanwhile she had left the horse to, more or less, his own devices when they reached a fence. Mark, being stronger and more apt to tell a horse where to jump rather than leave it to do its own thinking, had used the gag much more.

'It was the cause of all the trouble at Badminton,' he said. 'Columbus wasn't concentrating on where he was going; he was all the time thinking back to what I was doing. That first fall at the Luckington Lane fence at Badminton was a classic example. He had been used to being left to his own devices and, because of the gag and the fact that I was trying to place him at the fence, he wasn't thinking of the obstacle ahead – he was thinking, in some confusion, back to me.'

That particular Luckington Lane fence, consisting of rails at the edge of a bank, had a fearsome drop. Mark might well have broken a bone or two had his reactions not been tuned to the split second; fortunately he jumped off as Columbus, who had given the rails an almighty clout, went hurtling towards an abrupt collision with the Badminton pasture. He was to fall again, in the lake, before completing the course well down the field.

'After that,' said Mark, 'people kept telling me that I was a fool to ride such a dangerous horse. But I thought he was brilliant, despite the fact that I'd had a fall every time I'd ridden him. That year I had a five-pound bet with Mike Tucker that Columbus would finish in the top three at Badminton in 1974; I was rather sticking my neck out, because it takes some doing to get into the top three, but that's how much I thought of the horse.' Mike, with whom he was once in the Beaufort Pony Club, but he probably had qualms of conscience because his side of the bet seemed so akin to daylight robbery smilingly paid up the following year.

Meanwhile, back at the 1973 Badminton Championship, Princess Anne and Goodwill put up a commendable performance across country that was marred only by a technical refusal at the quarry. The horse had pecked at the bottom of the slide and landed on his nose, with the result that he missed the right-angled turn into a stone wall.

B

'I wasn't strong enough or quick enough to snatch him up and get round the corner,' said the Princess, 'partly because I'd been yanked too far out of the saddle.' She still finished in eighth place and, though over fifty points behind Lucinda Prior-Palmer who had won with exuberant ease on Be Fair, there was every reason to be satisfied. There was every reason, too, to believe that Goodwill would be capable of tackling the European Championships to be staged at Kiev later that year if Doublet, hoped to be on the road to complete recovery, should fail in fitness or performance during the final trial at Osberton.

Although almost everyone else connected with the sport – and many who knew scarcely anything at all about it – had decided that the Princess's defence of the European title rested solely on the recovery of Doublet, the Princess herself had considerable faith in Goodwill as an understudy: 'He didn't have as much experience as Doublet, but I still had tremendous confidence in him.'

In fact, Goodwill then seemed to be almost slanderously under-rated. Mark, who can produce a good stinging line in defence of horses thus treated, believes he is underrated still – 'It's because he doesn't do a poncy dressage test, which everyone can coo about, that people tend to run him down.'

But, although Princess Anne was worried about the prospect of Doublet jarring himself on the hard going that was known to be facing the British team horses in Kiev, Goodwill was still very much the understudy at the time of the final trial. He only got his part in the Kiev saga through the default of Doublet, who was eliminated for three refusals at one of Osberton's jumps into water.

'His legs were fine and he'd shown every sign of being back to his old self,' said Princess Anne. 'We'd been in water twice already that day. The first time was when we took the fastest route at a pole over a stream, which meant jumping it at an angle (I think I was the only person who did it that way) and Doublet never batted an eyelid until his legs disappeared into a patch of softness as he landed. We got out on to the bank, but in a heap because his feet were stuck: it seemed most unfortunate after he had jumped in so boldly.

'Then we had the log into the lake (which, in my humble

opinion, is one of the most unnecessary fences that's ever been built), and he jumped that well too. But after that I think he literally lost his nerve a bit and began to worry that his feet were going to disappear again as soon as he saw more water. He'd never stopped with me in his life before and I really didn't know what to do about it; he hadn't been naughty, he'd just seemed to freeze. The second time I thought he was going to jump, but the third time I knew he had absolutely no intention.'

So Doublet bowed out in sad ignominy and Goodwill was prepared for the journey to Kiev where Princess Anne, riding as an individual, was to defend her European title. Meanwhile Mark, without a suitable horse for the Championships, was preparing for an unexpected ride at Burghley, which took place the week before Kiev. He was to partner Maid Marion – in place of Bertie Hill's son, Tony, who was on the injured list – and it was only ten days before the event began that he tried the mare out for the first time.

Reporting on his cross-country round was to be fraught with *double entendres*. For how can one explain that the mare's tail was swishing with ominous resistance until half-way round the course, or that Mark's mixture of strength and sympathy finally won her submission, without hearing imaginary gales of raucous laughter from the uninitiated? Most of us who reported the event managed to steer a prim and evasive path through the minefield of double meanings but sub-editors still leapt on the little we had left them. The *Observer* was to appear the following morning with the headline: 'Captain Coaxes Maid'.

In fact, it had been one of the most impressive displays of horsemanship that I have ever seen – and the fact that it resulted in victory seemed entirely fitting. Riding any horse at the last moment is a formidable test of talent, but to get a good tune from one that happens to be in a thoroughly unco-operative mood deserves a surfeit of gushing superlatives.

Mark then flew out to Kiev, where he appeared in the role of a British supporter – but it was no ordinary, quietly anonymous role for he was, by now, officially engaged to Princess Anne, whose defence of the Individual European Championship had attracted maximum publicity because of her impending marriage. The defending British team was represented by Richard Meade on Wayfarer, Lucinda Prior-Palmer on Be Fair, Janet Hodgson on Larkspur and Debbie West on Baccarat.

The story of Kiev was to become, through a twist in the plot which none of the British riders anticipated, the melodrama of fence 2. Richard Meade, the sole man in the team, hadn't been concerned by it when walking the course, Mark had decided that he wouldn't bother to watch Princess Anne there but would station himself at a later fence; the Princess herself thought it was big but reasonably straightforward.

'I did think there was only one way to jump it,' she said, 'and that was my big mistake. It came in three sections and, if you came straight down the hill and aimed at the middle section, it presented a much better picture because there were more poles. Also it wasn't quite as wide and you could see it from further away so that the whole thing flowed on more easily. I simply didn't think there was any other way to jump it.

'But by the time that I came into the box at the end of the roads and tracks Baccarat and one or two other horses had had three refusals there, and word had come back that the bank in front of the middle section had started to crumble. So I was told to jump it on the left-hand side. Well, I couldn't really argue with that but, in retrospect, if I'd been a bit older and wiser, I would have said: "I'm sorry but I don't think I can because I haven't looked at the left-hand side." If ever there was a lesson to be learnt from Kiev, that was the lesson for me: it doesn't matter how straight-forward a fence may look, or how convinced you are about the way you're going to jump it, you must look at all the alternatives.

'It was one of those days when I had the special sort of "non-feeling" which I get from time to time. I don't feel frightened or confident or sick – in fact none of the things that I normally feel – I just feel dead. It normally indicates that something is going to go wrong, maybe that the horse is going to stop or that I'm going to fall off. It worried me a little in Kiev, but then I decided that the feeling resulted from having to change my plan regarding fence 2. I'd had the most super ride round the steeplechase course;

I wasn't particularly worried about the cross-country and I felt that the horse was going really well.

'The trouble with fence 2 was, basically, that I got it wrong. I had to ride along the side of a hill then make a right-angled turn to go down and into the fence. Unfortunately I hadn't gone far enough up the hill, so Goodwill didn't have enough forward speed to make the spread, He might just have done so had we met it plumb right, but I was half a stride out, so he had to stand a long way back from it.

'The interesting thing was that the horse didn't give me the impression that he thought he was going to hit it – and horses normally do, perhaps by leaving a leg behind or dropping their ears. We were a long way above the fence and, just as I was thinking: "Oh Lord, we're not going to make it", he literally dropped, just as though he'd hit a brick wall head on. His hind legs were already tucked up as far as they could go, so when his toes hit the far rail, he went bang, straight on his nose.

'It was like landing on tarmac as far as I was concerned. I had never ever hit the ground as hard or as fast. The main impact was on the side of my leg and, when I got up, it was numb from mid-thigh to mid-calf; I couldn't feel a thing. I wasn't, at that stage, aware that there was anything wrong with my shoulder, but I couldn't walk – I could stand on one leg and that was about all. I didn't think I'd broken anything, but Goodwill looked completely stunned and I couldn't walk, so I decided that there wasn't a great deal of point in going on. I was only riding as an individual, so there didn't seem to be a great deal of honour at stake – though that, of course, has since been disproved; apparently it should always be do or die.'

The last comment was directed, with a shaft of humour, towards her husband, with whom she had just had a spirited discussion on the perennial subject of injured or semi-conscious riders being pushed back into the saddle and told to ride on. It was to happen to Janet Hodgson, who was unable to see when legged up on to her horse in Luhmühlen in the 1975 European Championships. The Princess, arguing that Janet might have done serious damage to herself or to a spectator, thought this was carrying sport rather too far. Mark, who once played rugger for his school and is very much a team man rather than an individualist, believes in battling on to the last breath – 'for the sake of one's team and one's country'.

'Pooh to that,' said the Princess in appealingly un-Princess-like tones.

It says a great deal for their marriage that they can both weigh in hard and heavy with their own particular views without any hint of unpleasantness and without pulling any punches. As a mere spectator, I regarded it as a thoroughly wholesome indication of mutual respect.

In Kiev Janet Hodgson had staged her first do-or-die performance after (quite literally) biting the dust at fence 2. She wasn't pushed back in the saddle, she struggled there herself and, with four front teeth hanging by a thread of skin, she finished the course spectacularly bloodstained. But Janet was riding for the team, whereas Princess Anne was riding as an individual, and the Press reports that mentioned the two girls' efforts in snide juxtaposition failed to mention this elementary fact. There was probably a retaliatory element about such reporting for the journalistic grapevine, through which news circulates at the speed of Concorde, was already pumping through the story of the Princess's brush with photographers after her fall.

'I was accused of stomping over to them,' she said, 'but I couldn't stomp anywhere at the time. Actually, I didn't need to because they were all around me as I hobbled back to the stables. I did say: "So there you are, you've got what you wanted." As far as I was concerned it was merely a statement of fact.'

Unfortunately, photographers moving towards their subject *en masse* do tend to look like vultures moving in for the kill. There must have been some nice guys among the flock, who didn't particularly relish the moment, but individuals don't stand out in crowd scenes. And for anyone who is feeling sore and bruised and disappointed a gathering crowd is complete anathema.

During the course of that melodramatic day, fence 2 was to claim no less than thirty-five victims, statistically divided into twenty fallen and fifteen eliminated horses. The problem wasn't so much the fence itself, which consisted of a wide parallel over a gully, as the difficult approach, which stifled impulsion, and the fact that it came so early on, at a stage when horses hadn't really got going.

'Had it come half-way round the course,' said Mark, 'even in exactly the same place, I don't believe it would have caused much trouble.'

Considering the traumatic nature of Princess Anne's part in the drama, her retrospective thoughts on the event seemed startlingly favourable. 'To this day I feel terribly sorry for the Russians. The cross-country course was beautifully built and my only regret about not finishing was because it was such a very good course that I would liked to have ridden round it. Everyone was very kind, Kiev was fascinating and I personally had great fun; the only thing I wouldn't have recommended was the food. But it really was a good trip and, being me, what I liked most of all was the fact that we could zoom through Kiev in a mini-moke without anybody taking the slightest bit of notice.'

The Princess left Kiev on the morning after the final show jumping phase, in which Britain wound up in third place behind West Germany and Russia, with a Soviet rider, Alexander Evdokimov, relieving her of the individual title. She flew to Aberdeen with Prince Philip and, since her shoulder was then giving considerable pain, went to hospital for an X-ray. 'It was one of those ridiculous occasions,' she said, 'when the radiologist asked me to lie on my right-hand side and I replied: "Not bloody likely, that's the side that hurts." '

There were no cracks or breaks, which was entirely thanks to the fact that her leg had taken the brunt of the impact with Kiev's sun-baked ground. 'I was really extraordinarily lucky because I had almost dislocated my collar-bone,' she said, 'which, I'm told, is one of the most painful things that can happen. It had been pushed right up to the edge of the joint and it began to hurt as it was settling back into the socket. We then contacted a chap who's always putting my father together and he came up and spent five days working on me. I'd obviously torn a few ligaments and, to this day, my shoulders are slightly uneven.'

For a sizeable number of British riders, among them Princess Anne and Mark Phillips, the 1973 season was to end with a trip to Holland for the three-day event at Boekelo. And the event itself was to end in a desperately close finish, with Richard Meade on Wayfarer beating Mark on Laureate II by an infinitesimal margin.

Laureate was the up-and-coming horse of the year, whom many of us had been writing about with all the fulsomeness of a P.R. handout. He had won novice three-day events at Tidworth and Wylye; in a total of ten outings, since he embarked on the sport, he had never been out of the first two. Mark's Dutch trip was marred by the worry that this good young horse might not be quite ready for the substantial course that had been prepared in Boekelo: 'I couldn't decide whether I should pull up half-way round or keep going, so I didn't do a fast time.' Sadly, after jumping a clear round with consummate ease in Holland, Laureate developed leg trouble and then, in the summer of 1975, an infuriating habit of putting his tongue over the bit. Without the tongue to act as a cushion, the full pressure of the bit was exerted on the sensitive bars of the mouth; the reins in Mark's hands were therefore worse than useless.

But at Boekelo Laureate covered himself with glory, whereas Goodwill gave Princess Anne another fall. It wasn't a significant or painful fall; it was, in some ways, more of a comic sketch. The horse had been travelling fast and on his forehand when he had taken off too early, had his balance upset by brushing through the top of a fence, and landed on his nose. He then slid a considerable distance, on knees and nose, along the rain-soaked turf and, just when Princess Anne expected him to struggle to his feet, he keeled over.

'I rolled over and, when I leapt up to catch him, he was still lying on the ground,' she said. 'A Dutch girl, who had been waiting to grab his reins, was staring at him in dumb amazement. There was absolutely nothing wrong with him; it was that just he couldn't be bothered to get up. Goodwill had slid so far that I was convinced we must have been outside the penalty zone by the time he toppled over. We measured it later and thought we were right but, unfortunately, the Dutch hadn't marked the penalty zones so it was no help.'

Goodwill, who went on to complete the course in fine style, was therefore penalized for the fall and he finished well down the line. But the unofficial team, of which both Princess Anne and Mark were members, still won by a distance.

Then the engaged couple went home to prepare for their wedding. Many friends from three-day eventing were to be involved in the celebrations – while those who weren't dined out on the fact that they had rubbed shoulders with the Royal couple. All ways round it was a thoroughly joyous occasion.

11 | Triumph and tragedy

The most striking feature of the spring horse trials season of 1974 was the metamorphosis of Columbus. Headstrong and gauche a year earlier, he now looked so powerfully co-ordinated that one believed in his excellence almost before he had twitched a muscle to prove it. It was as though a Michelangelo fresco had been superimposed on a cave painting.

Mark had, of course, always carried the lines of the final picture in his imagination, but some time was to elapse before he was able to achieve it. The summer following the 1973 Badminton had left him precious little time for concentrated schooling; he was commuting between Germany, where he was on military manoeuvres, and England, where he was under a constant spotlight as the fiancé of Princess Anne. Even a jet-set exhibitionist might have decided it was all a bit too much.

And Mark is no exhibitionist. He is more the sort of person whom Jane Austen might have chosen for one of her heroes: considerate, honest and thoroughly genuine, the country gentleman rather than the city slicker. He is also a perfectionist, with the willpower that the term implies; when he was able to make regular visits to Alison Oliver's stable he was therefore utterly determined to uncover Columbus's enormous potential. The gag snaffle was discarded and the metamorphosis began.

In the advanced class of the one-day event at Liphook, three weeks before the start of the 1974 Badminton Championship, Princess Anne and Mark were to prove themselves, competitively speaking, a formidable married couple. Mark won on Columbus and finished third on Great Ovation; Princess Anne finished second on a very fit-looking Doublet. These three horses, plus Goodwill, were to give them two rides apiece in the Badminton classic and Liphook was part of their preparation.

'I'm afraid I use one-day events as a means to an end rather than as actual competitions,' said Princess Anne. 'I may get rather competitive when I get there, but I don't think about it beforehand very much. I'm always very pleased if the horse gets round and goes well, because that's the main object of the exercise.

'The one-day events bring the horses on a tremendous amount; they concentrate the mind wonderfully. It's very difficult when you're schooling to think of enough variety and you don't always ask the right questions. So I tend to rely on events like Liphook to get me up to scratch.'

Marriage had, as it were, given the Royal couple the chance to pool their talents. Mark's forte was the cross-country ('though I wouldn't say I enjoyed it the most – it used to frighten the living daylights out of me!'); Princess Anne's was the dressage. Cynics might add that dressage happens to be the only area in which the judges can show a certain amount of partiality towards the Royal participant, but it would be patently unfair to suggest that the majority of her performances with Doublet were anything less than excellent. She may, on occasion, have been generously marked with Goodwill, who sometimes looks uncomfortably like a volcano on the brink of eruption, but other well-known competitors have been known to receive generous marks as well.

'I think it happens the world over,' said Mark, 'that if, say, Richard Meade is coming in to do a test, the judges expect it to be good and so they are thinking in sevens and eights. If it were a complete unknown they'd be more likely to think in fives and sixes.'

The Princess took up the theme: 'I don't believe the judges think: "Oh gracious, here comes Princess Anne." '

'Poppycock!' said her husband, cheerfully.

'What I mean is that they probably associate me with good dressage marks and that's what they're thinking about, as opposed to HRH.'

'But there was a particular judge who once gave you some quite *extraordinary* marks at Badminton!'

He didn't need to tell his wife that he meant the marks were extraordinarily generous, so she replied with her favourite retort: 'I think that *you* need to be very careful in what you say about dressage judges because, when they see you in your smart uniform, you get ten marks just for the salute. It's perfectly true, and we both know it, that there are certain lady judges (who shall remain nameless) who have also been known to give *you* some extraordinary marks.'

It is also, of course, perfectly true that there is no dressage judge in the world who could hope to gain the wholehearted approval of all the *cognoscenti* gathered round the arena. There has to be an element of personal preference for a particular type of horse – and there may even be a subconscious bias in favour of Royal titles or smart uniforms or whatever – but the judges have to be given the credit for doing their best to be objective. If we were debarred from slating them, however, the dressage phase would lose much of its piquancy.

As usual, Mark made his final preparations for Badminton with Bertie Hill at South Molton. This time Princess Anne went with him and, because they had taken only one groom, she looked after Doublet herself. Her European Championship partner was always very aloof in the stable, and though she would have welcomed a greater show of interest, it made him that much easier to muck out, groom and feed.

'It was almost the first time I'd ever looked after a horse,' she said, 'because I'd never really had the opportunity when I was driving to and fro from Alison's. I thoroughly enjoyed it, despite being constantly worried that Doublet wouldn't look as well or eat as much as when the girl was looking after him.'

In fact, he looked marvellously well for the dressage phase of Badminton, where there was nothing in the least extraordinary about the marks which left him in the lead at the end of that phase. Mark was lying second on Great Ovation and equal third on Columbus, while Goodwill, their only disappointment, was a rather lowly twenty-seventh. But cross-country day, always an occasion for great reshufflings and more than a little drama, was to play its customary role.

The first upset came when Great Ovation was eliminated for three refusals at the Bullfinch. Had it occurred to Mark that the horse might conceivably have dug in his toes at this particular fence, he would have ridden into it with considerably more gusto. But the first refusal came as a bolt from the blue and, being in close proximity to the preceding fence, the Bullfinch became far more difficult when tackled for the second time. Lacking the space to attack this typical hunting fence at typical hunting pace, Mark had two more refusals with his dual Badminton winner and Great Ovation dropped out in disgrace.

But with Columbus it was quite a different story. The big grey, controlled and foot perfect every inch of the way, ate up the cross-country course in long ground-eating strides and moved to the top of the class. It was a round of inspired virtuosity that left those of us who were reporting the event struggling (mostly in vain) for suitably eloquent phrases with which to describe it.

Meanwhile, Goodwill had proved his capabilities – and confounded his critics – with a splendidly accurate clear round across country that was to leave Princess Anne in fifth place at the end of the day. But Doublet, the overnight leader, sadly dropped out on the steeplechase course. He had carved his way through the open ditch and fallen with awesome ferocity; Princess Anne, having spent some two and a half years waiting for Doublet to reproduce some semblance of his European Championship form, must have plumbed the depths of depression as she retired him from the contest.

Joy and tribulation are a familiar mixture for anyone involved with horses; they had come in close proximity in the course of a single day in which both members of the family had achieved one fine performance and both had suffered one disaster. But the final show jumping day was unclouded. Columbus jumped a clear round to give Mark his third Badminton victory (this time over Janet Hodgson on Larkspur and the United States rider Bruce Davidson on Irish Cap); Goodwill was also clear and he edged up in the placings to finish fourth.

Mark had been unbeaten in British three-day events since the previous May; he had won at Tidworth and Wylye on Laureate

II, at Burghley on Maid Marion and at Badminton on Columbus. Yet another win at Tidworth the following month on Persian Holiday was to make it an incredible 'five-timer', which will surely never be achieved again.

Mark describes the competition between himself and his wife in straightforward terms: 'Certainly there's the will to win (we both have that), but if we have to be beaten by anyone, we'd much rather be beaten by each other.'

'It's easy for him to say that because he's normally in a higher place anyway,' said the Princess, in a bantering tone that implied she agreed with him.

Mark was away on military manoeuvres shortly after winning his third Badminton Championship, while the Princess was working with Doublet, who was by then stabled at Sandhurst and was due to compete at Tidworth. It was May, which is not always such a merry month as some poets would have us suppose, and in 1974 it was to bring swift and unexpected tragedy.

Doublet had shown no apparent ill effects from his fall at Badminton; had he been lame he might well have been X-rayed – and both the Princess and Alison believe that an X-ray would have revealed a star fracture above the hock on his hind leg. But, when they set out together to ride in Windsor Great Park, there was no hint of the tragedy to come.

Princess Anne describes that morning as 'quite the most ghastly experience of my entire life'. She had been cantering across Smith's Lawn when she heard the sickening sound of her horse's leg breaking, so she pulled him up and dismounted. Doublet, proud and aloof to the last, put his head down and grazed, while Princess Anne stood by, agonized by her total inability to do anything that might help him. She waited until Alison, then at least a mile away, came to see what was wrong; she waited even longer until a vet could be brought to the scene.

'When the vet arrived,' she said, 'he started explaining that there was nothing he could do for the horse. I wasn't able to speak at the time, but if I had been able to, I would have said, "Yes, I know, so *please* get on with it." '

On that May morning her horse was put down.

12 | Columbus at the World Championships

The 1974 Army Horse Trials at Tidworth very nearly resulted in Mark Phillips and Princess Anne achieving a record husband and wife double. Both were leading their respective sections as they went into the final show jumping phase – but, whereas Mark went on to victory with Persian Holiday, Princess Anne's single mistake on Flame Gun dropped her back to second place behind Aly Pattinson on Olivia.

It was the memory of Doublet's broken leg, which had occurred earlier that week and remained excruciatingly vivid, that was the main contributory factor to Flame Gun's defeat. On the steeple-chase course the Princess had suddenly felt that her young horse had also done some damage to a leg and she pulled him up before realizing that it was just an illusion. 'I thought he'd broken down,' she said, 'because he wasn't galloping properly, but he seemed to regain his balance when I trotted him.' Flame Gun went on to prove his well-being with a fast cross-country round, unpenalized by either jumping or time penalties, but the steeplechase stoppage had cost him 5.6 penalties and he was defeated, in the end, by just 2.7 points.

Princess Anne was not exactly overjoyed by the final result. 'I find it very irritating to be second,' she said. 'In many ways I'd much rather be third or fourth.'

But it was her husband who had to swallow quite the nastiest three-day event pill dished out that year, during the World Championship staged at Burghley. Preparations for the big event had been fraught with problems. A month before the Championship Mark jigged up his old back injury which stems from his school athletic days; then Columbus knocked a leg in the horsebox *en route* to the final trial at Osberton and, because of slight lameness, couldn't be seen in action. The selectors, who normally commit themselves immediately after the final trial in the belief that a firm decision makes for a better atmosphere during training, decided to play for time. They therefore picked six riders from whom four would be nominated for the team on the eve of the competition. Mark was naturally one of the six, but the delaying tactics indicated the selectors' concern regarding his own and his partner's fitness; if doubts lingered on for another week they would have to go as individuals (assuming they were able to go at all) rather than as team members. Horse and rider were, however, seen to be working well together during the crucial period of decision and were therefore included on the team – together with Richard Meade on Wayfarer II, Chris Collins on Smokey VI and Bridget Parker on Cornish Gold. Nine full teams were to compete in opposition: Austria, France, Germany, Ireland, Italy, Poland, Switzerland, USA and USSR. There were individual entries from Canada and the Netherlands, while Britain's eight individuals included Princess Anne on Goodwill.

So the stage was set for a ding-dong battle, in which Burghley House was to provide an elegant backcloth to performances that ranged from comedy to tragedy, from mediocrity to virtuosity in the course of a single day. And that, of course, was cross-country day.

Columbus played the role of virtuoso once again; unpenalized on the steeplechase course, he sailed over Bill Thompson's admirable cross-country course of thirty-two fences in the majestic manner that befitted a horse of Royal ownership and he achieved the fastest time of the day to take over the lead. It was only between the last two fences that there was any hint that Columbus might end up in the role of a wounded hero. Trying to piece those moments together afterwards, Mark decided the damage must have occurred as he accelerated away from the penultimate fence.

'I didn't know what had happened at the time,' he said. 'I thought it was just a bandage that had slipped, so I tried to have a look but I couldn't see anything; then the last fence was on top

F

of us.' He cleared the last, rode the short distance to the finish and dismounted. The discovery that Columbus's bandages were still securely in place was full of ominous implications that were proved only too depressingly well founded: he had slipped part of a tendon off his hock. It was an unusual problem in that tendons, if they slip at all, normally break away from the hock completely whereas Columbus's was still partially attached to the joint.

The full veterinary facts, however, were to emerge fairly slowly. When the horse was examined on his return to the stables after the cross-country, it was with the hope that he might yet be fit to take part in the final show jumping phase the following day.

'We weren't very pleased with the two vets,' said Princess Anne. 'They wouldn't communicate with each other and they both said different things. One said: "Put on a hot compress"; the other said, "Put on a cold compress." It really didn't help matters very much.'

But, by the time the veterinary inspection was due to begin the following morning, Columbus was sound and everyone's hopes took an upward surge. Alas, they were to plummet soon afterwards when Columbus kicked out – ironically enough at the British team vet, Peter Scott-Dunn – and damaged the same tendon yet again. He was never an angel in the stable. 'Like most brilliant horses,' said Mark, who thinks the world of him, 'he'd kick you as soon as look at you.'

That particular kick marked the end of Columbus's involvement in the 1974 World Championships – though, in retrospect, it is highly unlikely that he would have managed the show jumping anyway. But it was a bitter disappointment to Mark. Most riders have experienced the frustrations of a horse going lame at an inopportune moment, but to have an individual championship so cruelly wrenched from his grasp represented a good few extra turns of the screw. The long-term implications were equally depressing. 'One moment I realized that I was riding a horse that was probably the best in the world,' said Mark, 'and the next moment I realized that I might never have the chance to compete with him again.'

Columbus's lameness belonged in the same bracket as the misfortune of the Queen Mother's horse, Devon Loch, who crumpled up on the flat when he looked to have the 1956 Grand National safely in his pocket. Mark, however, would be the first to testify that he was by no means home and dry when he had to pull out. Bruce Davidson, who eventually won the title on Irish Cap, had been only eight points behind Columbus, while his compatriot, Michael Plumb, on Good Mixture, was just a couple of decimal points further back. The two Americans (coincidentally, the first two to be mentioned by Mark and the Princess when they were asked to name the riders whom they most admire) were therefore less than the cost of one show jumping error behind the lost British hope. But Columbus had, after all, jumped clear in the last phase at Badminton and there is no reason to suppose that he wouldn't have done the same in the World Championships.

The Queen's other horse, Goodwill, also required veterinary treatment at the end of cross-country day. He had thrown an enormous leap at the open ditch on the steeplechase course before virtually pulling up a stride or two away. Once again the memory of Doublet's death was evoked with awesome clarity.

'For a moment it felt as though he'd really broken something badly and I thought: "Oh Lord, not again." It was terrifying,' said Princess Anne. 'I let him trot for a while and he somehow sorted himself out, but he didn't set off across country in his usual way and he didn't jump anything like as freely as he normally does. I was worried all the way round because, although he wasn't lame, I had the feeling that something was hurting him.'

Goodwill had one totally uncharacteristic refusal at the Double Coffin and he gave Princess Anne a few awful imitations of a nose-diving Spitfire during the rest of their journey. 'The two drop fences, the Dairy Mound and Waterloo Rails, were really quite frightening,' she said. 'He didn't seem to jump them so much as to drop off the edge and go straight down. Then we very nearly fell at the water. He left one leg on the other side of the fence and was virtually perpendicular as he went in, but he managed to get his legs disentangled just in time. It was really very clever of him because he should have landed slap on his face.'

In retrospect, the Princess believes that Goodwill must have given himself an almighty thump on the steeplechase course. Fortunately, the blow was on the back of the tendon sheath rather than at the side where it might have inflicted incurable injury, but it still caused a good deal of concern to Peter Scott-Dunn who was treating him that evening.

The scoreboard gave no indication of all the anxieties surrounding Goodwill's effort. It merely recorded that he had incurred twenty penalties for a refusal, which was widely regarded as an insignificant but unfortunate error, and that he had moved up from a lowly forty-second after the dressage to stand fifteenth at the end of the cross-country phase. He was to edge a little higher after the final show jumping, in which he incurred just a half penalty on time, to collect the last of the twelve prizes.

Another of the British individuals, Hugh Thomas on Playamar, stood third, behind America's Bruce Davidson and Michael Plumb, while Britain finished second to the United States in the team placings. The transatlantic threat had been preceded by warning shots in three consecutive Olympic Games; this time the Americans would have won the team title even if Columbus had been fit enough for the final phase.

13 | An all-female team

At the beginning of 1975, Princess Anne spent most of her time in the stables. She and Mark then had five horses at Sandhurst, and only one girl to look after them, so she had decided to 'do' two of them herself. There was no delegating of the less glamorous stable work; the Princess mucked out, fed and groomed her two horses, as well as exercising both of them and working the others. She also cleaned their tack, which is a chore that Mark detests.

Her spell as girl groom lasted for about two months and she looks back on it with satisfaction: 'I think it's good for one and I think you get to know the horses much better. In fact, I now rather resent not being able to look after the horses I ride.'

'It may be slightly sentimental,' said Mark, 'but I think if you can look after your own horses it's a tremendous advantage.'

The trouble is that it happens to be a full-time job. Unless they are short of grooms, the Royal couple like to limit each girl's responsibility to two horses. 'People say it's crazy,' said Mark, 'but we have to be away on certain days and, when that happens, the girls do the exercising. If they're riding twice a morning – say from eight until ten o'clock and again from ten-thirty to twelve-thirty – their morning's gone. If they had to ride in the afternoon as well, there wouldn't be time for the stable-work.'

Princess Anne was not only riding twice a morning during 1975 and doing stable-work, she was also helping to prepare Mark's horses for Badminton while he was away on military exercises. The girls coped with most of the early preparations, when Mark's horses came up from grass and started their daily two hours of walking on the roads at the end of January, and

they helped with the straightforward exercising. But as always
the Princess and Mark did the cantering and galloping, the dressage and the jumping themselves. If one of them was away from
home, the other cantered all the horses in training at Sandhurst.

Both believe that they have complemented each other since
their marriage. 'I think my dressage has improved no end,' said
Mark, 'and I think Princess Anne's cross-country has also improved.'

('That's because he's forever yelling that I'm not going fast
enough!')

Mark ignored the badinage. 'I think she's definitely changed
her approach to riding across country and, because she rides all
the horses, I think she's had an effect on their dressage. She's
very, very quiet and tactful and sensitive, and therefore very
good at making the horses relax.'

'But I'm not as even-tempered as Mark,' said the Princess. 'We
both lose our tempers occasionally – and sometimes Mark worse
than me – but, normally speaking, he's a very even-tempered
rider. When I get annoyed, I tend to yell at the horses just to
inform them that I'm thoroughly displeased, but it doesn't have
much effect! We've decided on occasions (especially when things
aren't working out right and we're getting a bit annoyed) that
it helps to put the other jockey on the horse. Mark says that I'm
relaxed but, if I've been worried about something and he gets
on one of my horses, the same thing applies. The jockey who
isn't riding the horse in the competition tends to be far more
relaxed and less fussed about whatever problem has arisen.'

The three months of preparation for the 1975 Badminton proved
a damp and abortive effort for everyone concerned; after weeks
of rain had made the ground in Badminton Park as soft as a wet
sponge, the event was abandoned at the end of the first day of
dressage. Princess Anne had been planning to ride Goodwill in
his third Badminton; Mark had entered Laureate II and Persian
Holiday for the first time, but withdrawn both of them shortly
before the abbreviated event began. With both horses out of
action through slight lameness, the cancellation made little difference to his own plans.

It mattered much more to those whose up-and-coming horses had been declared for the Championship, since they were thus denied the opportunity of proving their talents in time to be considered for the 1975 European Championships. The selectors were also handicapped, for it meant that they would have to take the well-being of the seasoned campaigners on trust and select their team on the previous year's form; the talented youngsters would have to wait for another year.

Mark, however, had one remaining chance of proving that Laureate II was worthy of a place, for he and Princess Anne were among a small contingent of British riders travelling to the United States that summer for the Ledyard Farm three-day event in Massachusetts. Both he and the Princess, who was to finish tenth on Arthur of Troy, believed that Laureate was ready to make an impressive comeback after his year on the sidelines.

'The horse had never seemed as well or been going better,' said Mark. 'But we left him standing in the horsebox for a while, without thinking that the sound from the loudspeakers might upset him. But he's a slightly sensitive horse and I think he must have got wound up, started playing with the bit in his mouth and got his tongue over it. That day I had a terrible ride on him, over the steeplechase and the cross-country, and it was totally out of character. Eventually we were eliminated for three refusals at the Coffin.'

The trouble wasn't immediately diagnosed and there were those who maintained that the horse wasn't properly fit or that he was affected by the heat. Neither explanation seemed in the least convincing. 'Almost the only person who made any sense,' said Princess Anne, 'was Janet Hodgson, who was over there with Gretna Green. She'd had a horse that used to get its tongue over the bit and she was convinced that Laureate was doing the same.'

Janet was proved right, but it was too late for the horse to redeem his reputation. The selectors were naturally more interested in Harley, who had finished second with Sue Hatherly behind World Champion Bruce Davidson on Golden Griffin, and in Ben Wyvis, whom Mike Tucker had ridden into fifth place. Mike was to become the only man among the six British riders to compete for the European Championships at Luhmühlen in West Germany, where he and Carolan Geekie competed as individuals.

The British team was, for the first time, all-female: Princess Anne on Goodwill, Janet Hodgson on Larkspur, Sue Hatherly on Harley and Lucinda Prior-Palmer on Be Fair.

Naturally, there was much discussion on the well-worn subject of whether women are tough enough, both mentally and physically, for an international three-day event. The story of Australia's Bill Roycroft was told for the umpteenth time, of how he broke his shoulder on the cross-country course in the 1960 Olympic three-day event, remounted to finish the course *and* discharged himself from hospital in order to jump a clear round in the show jumping phase and so win a team gold medal.

Frank Weldon's much quoted line ('Women should be at home warming somebody's slippers') was given another airing – and this time, he says, his words were reported accurately. In earlier Press Room bantering, Frank had vehemently denied that he had ever said they should be home warming their *husbands'* slippers. Unrepentant of his statement, he was to become one of the arch-enemies of Women's Lib by saying, on a pre-Badminton television programme in 1976, that girls are less fitted to cope with the strains and stresses of a major competition: 'When something goes wrong, there's a little tear and a little sniff.'

Mark's views are probably not far removed from Frank Weldon's – though he doesn't talk about tears or sniffs. He believes that the success of the British girls merely reflects the fact that there are many more of them taking part: 'If you look at the number of men competing at Badminton and the proportion of them that finish in the top ten, it's a much more impressive percentage than for the girls!' He too has reservations about the girls' mental and physical strength.

Princess Anne, though certainly no Women's Libber, doesn't accept the whole of his argument: 'I can't think why you should believe that women are less good at coping with psychological pressures. Surely it depends on the person, not on whether they're male or female.'

Eridge, 1971. 'I was saying to myself: "Well, it feels all right at the moment . . ." '

Eridge, 1971. 'Doublet led after the dressage, but he was a bit bold going through that funny water jump.'

Goodwill at Kiev, 1973. 'We were a long way above the fence and, just as I was thinking: "Oh Lord, we're not going to make it", he literally dropped . . . . It was like landing on tarmac as far as I was concerned.'

Flame Gun at Amberley,
1973 (*right*) and Good-
will at Badminton, 1974.
Below: Engagement
photograph (left to right)
Prince Philip, Mark,
Princess Anne, Anne
Phillips, the Queen and
Peter Phillips.

Two horses that contributed to Mark's 'five-timer' in British three-day events. Persian Holiday (*right*) was subsequently short-listed for the Montreal Olympics, but Laureate II was eliminated in the United States where the picture below was taken – 'I think he must have got wound up, started playing with the bit in his mouth and got his tongue over it.'

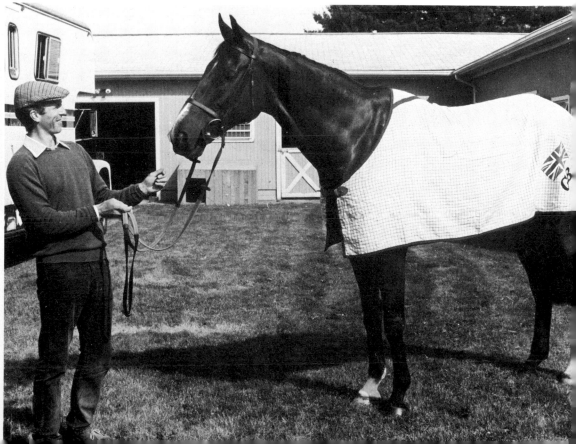

Above: Columbus playing the role of virtuoso in the 1974 World Championships, before finishing the course as a wounded hero. 'I thought it was just a bandage that had slipped,' said Mark.

OPPOSITE PAGE: Badminton, 1973. Columbus kept his dispiriting record for the spring season intact by falling not once, but twice. 'After that people kept telling me that I was a fool to ride such a dangerous horse,' said Mark. 'But I thought he was brilliant.' In 1974 (*below*), Mark and Columbus won the Badminton Championship.

Lucinda Prior-Palmer (*left*) and Janet Hodgson, individually tenth and fourth in the 1974 World Championships. *Below:* The winning United States team (left to right): Michael Plumb on Good Mixture, Denny Emerson on Victor Dakin, Don Sachey on Plain Sailing and Bruce Davidson on Irish Cap. The Americans would have won the team title even if Columbus had been fit enough for the final phase.

She does, however, concede the question of physical strength. 'I'm forever muttering that it's all very well for him; he can *make* his horses do certain things by using his legs and hands because he's very strong, whereas I have to think of some other way. I have to con them – and I'm sure girls find that there are certain horses that are particularly "connable" to them.'

This is the main reason why most leading ladies, in both show jumping and eventing, have built their reputation through one exciting and marvellously sympathetic partnership. One of the rare exceptions is Caroline Bradley who – through her stylish, quiet and sympathetic riding – has coaxed a fine tune from a variety of different horses and is now the show jumping rider whom Princess Anne most admires.

When I asked the Princess whether it might not have been easier to have a man or two on the team, Mark interjected with: 'It's more than her life is worth to admit it!'

But she did, nevertheless, say that she was glad to have Mike Tucker among the British contestants. 'He is very good value. I would have to admit that, if all six of us had been female, it might have been rather different. But Mike is a character and it was great fun to have him there; he cuts everyone down to size which is very good for one.'

Mike is a working farmer, with a good sense of fun and a natural spontaneity. He had ridden Laurieston to victory at Tidworth the year before Richard Meade won team and individual gold medals on the horse; twelve months prior to that he had won at Tidworth with another of Derek Allhusen's home-bred horses, Laureate (not to be confused with Mark's mount, Laureate II). Mike celebrated his first Tidworth win with characteristic generosity by buying a drink for almost everyone in sight, including a few thirsty journalists.

The 1975 European Championships were officially opened on the eve of the first day of dressage, in the old market place of Lüneburg, a few miles from Luhmühlen. The ten chefs d'équipe (from Bulgaria, West Germany, Russia, Great Britain, Ireland, Italy, Poland, France, the Netherlands and Switzerland) had been asked to dress like the members of their team – which for Britain's

Colonel Bill Lithgow, had he taken the request seriously, would have meant appearing in drag.

'There were a few problems about that,' said Princess Anne, 'and a lot of funny ideas, especially when it came to deciding what we would make Tucker wear!'

At the opening ceremony, Mike Tucker looked rather as though he had tagged on to the wrong team. The five girls standing in a line on his right were lithe and trim in their blouses, skirts and high-heeled shoes; they presented so striking a contrast to the other teams that they would have been the centre of attraction even had Princess Anne not been in their midst. Except for the British and the Irish, who had one woman on their team and one riding as an individual, it was an all-male field.

For the British team, narrowly ahead after two days of dressage, the cross-country was to begin disastrously with two falls for poor Janet Hodgson and Larkspur. Princess Anne, second to go for the team, set out at about ten o'clock in the morning feeling distinctly groggy.

'I had the most appalling cold,' she said, 'though I don't think anyone realized it at the time. I was so blocked up that I'd hardly slept a wink the night before and I was beginning to feel that it was all quite ghastly. It was just before I started on the steeplechase that I heard about Janet's first fall and that put the fear of God into me, because I knew I would have to get a move on.'

The steeplechase course was shaped like a figure-of-eight with an extra loop on one side. 'It was very exciting,' said the Princess, 'because you couldn't relax for a second; you had to keep remembering when to turn across the middle. When we finished I was very pleased with Goodwill; I don't think the old boy has ever gone so fast in his life.'

By the time Janet's second fall was announced she was 'feeling slightly more awake'. The unwelcome news did at least resolve one problem about which she had been plagued with indecision: 'There was a fence that I might have taken by the short way because it suited Goodwill, but I realized there was no question of that when I heard about Janet – I would have to play for safety and take it by the longer route.'

The Princess looked supremely calm as she waited to start the cross-country phase. 'Perhaps my limited advantage is an ability to relax at competitions,' she said, as though it was a perfectly natural reflex. It wasn't an ability that was much in evidence among the other riders, most of whom seemed to have the thirty big, solid cross-country fences very much in mind as they prepared to start. But Princess Anne looked as though she was simply saying goodbye to her friends before setting off on a pleasant hack.

'I thought I set off rather faster than usual,' she said, 'though Mark doesn't agree. I was actually kicking to begin with and I gave Goodwill a slap before we reached the water because his mind didn't seem to be quite with it.'

The water, fence 6, was a complex combination, that offered two alternative routes. Like most of the other riders, except the West Germans, Princess Anne took it on the right: over the post and rails and the stream, up the bank and over an upturned boat into a stretch of water, out on to another bank and over the trellis. There were to be five falls at this complex by the end of the day and, for one nasty moment, it looked as though Goodwill might also lose his rider there.

'I thought he was going to stand off to jump the boat,' said Princess Anne, 'but he didn't; he put in a short one and just popped over.' The result was not particularly elegant but the Princess's natural balance stood her in good stead. She galloped on at a rattling pace, along the sandy tracks that ran through a forest of pine trees.

The other difficult complex came near the end of the course at fences 23, 24 and 25. This comprised a hedge, followed by a short right-angled turn into a tree trunk, with a Normandy Bank only a few strides beyond it. Fifteen horses (including Harley), finding themselves faced with the tree trunk immediately after the turn, refused there. Goodwill, equally short of space, went ahead and jumped it.

'He has the show jumper's ability to fold up his front legs,' said Princess Anne. 'If there is a fence where he has to turn a bit sharp and come in a bit close, it doesn't worry him; he doesn't panic about it. He had his front feet right under that tree trunk in Luhmühlen, but he still jumped it – and he went on over the Normandy Bank, although he was taking it virtually from a standstill.'

Twelve of the fourteen horses who preceded Goodwill had managed to complete the course, but all of them finished in a tired canter. So few of us will forget the stirring moment when Princess Anne emerged on the home straight, with Goodwill still going like an express train. She had kicked on after the Normandy Bank and the horse had found an extra gear. 'He was enjoying himself,' she said. 'It was very much his sort of course. I didn't have to yank and pull to slow him up before fences; he could take them very much as he came to them and I think he appreciated that. I thought it was a lovely course.'

Having dismounted and weighed out, there was a spontaneous hug and a kiss from Mark, which the BBC Television commentator, Dorian Williams, described with true-blue British dignity as 'a well deserved reward'.

The rest of the Luhmühlen story is now old history. Lucinda Prior Palmer, who conjured up another inspired British performance on Be Fair, won the individual gold medal, while Princess Anne won the silver and thus became the first woman since Sheila Willcox, the European Champion of 1957, to achieve international success with two different horses. Mike Tucker, showing that he wasn't only there to provide light relief, finished seventh on Ben Wyvis. Though the show jumping fall of poor Sue Hatherly and Harley robbed the team of a gold medal and replaced it with a silver, no one could deny that the *Britischen Amazonen* had done a splendid job. They deserved all the fulsome praise bestowed on them by the German Press.

When they returned home Mark was left with just a few days to prepare for the Burghley Horse Trials. He was to partner Brazil, whom he had ridden for the first time just a few days before travelling out to Luhmühlen, and Gretna Green, whom he hadn't ridden at all. He was offered the last-minute ride on Gretna only two days before Burghley started because the mare's owner,

Janet Hodgson, was still suffering from concussion after her two falls in Germany.

Both horses jumped clear rounds over the cross-country, which some observers regarded as more difficult than Luhmühlen, and they thus reaffirmed Mark's rare talents as a horseman. Gretna Green eventually finished second, beaten only by Aly Pattinson on Carawich, and Brazil, who missed a place among the prize-winners through three show jumping mistakes, was sixteenth.

'I've been very lucky,' said Mark, 'in that various people have asked me to ride their horses at different times and I've been only too happy to do so. There's a tremendous amount of difference between somebody ringing me up without any prompting and the selectors asking: "Can we have your horse for Mark Phillips to ride?" I've always thought it rather unfair to put people in a position where they feel they ought to lend their horse although they enjoy riding it themselves. There was once a suggestion that I should try and persuade a rider to lend me a particular horse for the European Championships and I said: "You must be joking!" If the person concerned hadn't been happy on the horse and had wanted to lend it, that would have been quite different a story. I certainly wasn't going to wade in and try to lure a horse off anybody.'

Princess Anne, a spectator at Burghley, was back in the saddle two weeks later for the Bramham three-day event, where she rode her six-year-old Mardi Gras, a chestnut gelding by Manicou, into third place in the Griffin Section. It was a slightly galling result, since she would have won the class very comfortably but for losing concentration at one of the easiest cross-country fences and thus incurring twenty penalties for a refusal.

The Princess's final appearance in a horsy setting during 1975 was in front of the television cameras, when she took part in a *Blue Peter* programme featuring handicapped riders. She had become Patron of the Riding for the Disabled Association in 1972, through the Duchess of Norfolk who was already its hard-working President, and has since visited groups all over the country, talking to disabled riders and those who help them.

She has learnt to admire the guts of the riders (many of whom are lifted from a wheelchair to a saddle); she is aware that the exercise can strengthen wasted muscles and, above all, she sees the pleasure derived by those who regard the weekly ride as the highlight of their lives. 'I'd always thought that riding for the disabled must be a good idea,' she said, 'but now I'm totally convinced of it.'

'Mark is the stable management expert,' said Princess Anne. 'That side's a complete mystery to me.'

It wasn't quite true, of course, since the Princess is thoroughly conversant with all the stable routine, but it meant that her husband makes the decisions with regard to the amount of food and exercise each horse should have.

'I'd hardly call myself an expert,' said Mark, 'but I think I apply a certain amount of commonsense to looking after horses. Some people underdo them – they just chuck hay and oats into the stable and hope for the best. Conversely, some people overdo them and feed practically every vitamin on the market; it becomes an endless teaspoon of this and teaspoon of that until the horse is like a walking chemist's shop.

'I think we probably try to steer somewhere in the middle and we do rather pride ourselves on the fact that our horses always look well. We feed on a day-to-day basis which means, in its simplest form, that if a horse comes out of its stable bucking and kicking we tend to cut down on its oats and give it more work. If it comes out looking lethargic we try and find out what's wrong. It may be that the horse has a vitamin deficiency or it may simply mean that he's having too much work and not enough to eat.'

In the first few months of 1976 Mark was applying his commonsense to the management of six horses. His own mounts, Brazil, Persian Holiday and Laureate II, plus his wife's Flame Gun and Arthur of Troy, were being prepared for a possible attempt at the Badminton Championship; by early February Goodwill was plodding round the roads near Sandhurst in preparation for a later seasonal debut. Two more of Mark's Badminton prospects, Columbus and Favour, had begun their training in Alison Oliver's yard.

Columbus was clearly the horse more than any other that Mark would have wished to ride and, since the Queen's big grey had progressed well since his operation, everybody's fingers were tightly crossed. 'We were quite hopeful until the beginning of March,' said Alison, 'but, when we increased the work, he began to be more unlevel and we then realized that his eventing career was over. So he was turned out to grass at Hampton Court.'

Mark's string of Badminton possibles was therefore reduced to four. He wouldn't be able to compete with more than three of them, but numerical strength is an obvious asset in a sport which depends so much on the soundness and well-being of the horses. Whereas Princess Anne had been told (after her European Championship silver medal) that the selectors didn't require Goodwill to compete at Badminton, Mark was back in the position, familiar to all top-class riders, of having to prove that he had a mount of Olympic calibre. Badminton was therefore of crucial importance.

The preparatory three months were naturally hectic. As Mark pointed out: 'If you want to be at the top in an amateur sport you have to devote a tremendous amount of time to it; that's why there's so much shamateurism. You either need financial assistance or a very benevolent boss who will give you the time to train.' Fortunately for him, the Army does tend to be fairly benevolent to anyone who has reached the top rung of the ladder in an amateur sport, especially during an Olympic year. Fortunately, also, he had his wife to help him.

A fairly typical day, which took place about a month before the 1976 Badminton Championship, involved a journey to Windsor Great Park for Princess Anne, her husband and four of their horses. There they rode two horses apiece, starting with half to three-quarters of an hour of dressage with each one. They then did some cantering. Four circuits around the polo pitches on Smith's Lawn, ridden at an easy and relaxed canter, doesn't sound too strenuous until you discover that the four circuits involve a distance of approximately five miles. And at the end of their first five-mile canter, they both leapt on to another horse and did the same again.

'It's the best way of getting fit,' said the Princess, without a sign of a wince. 'If you have the horses to do that type of work, it's the best preparation you can have. One horse on its own doesn't really get you fit enough.'

The Royal horsebox, driven by either Mark or the Princess, had become a familiar sight to those on duty at the barrier to the grounds of the Royal Military Academy, Sandhurst. But it didn't mean that the metal arm swung upwards as soon as the vehicle came in sight. 'Sometimes,' said the Princess, 'they seem to forget that there are only two lunatics who drive horseboxes in this part of the world and I happen to be one of them!'

Another familiar sight was that of the Princess knuckling down to stablework. 'Mucking out and cleaning tack, that's all I ever seem to do in the stables nowadays,' she told me that March. 'It helps to cut down the work for the girls who are looking after the horses.'

Flame Gun was – and doubtless still is – one of her favourites in the stable. 'He's a character,' she said. 'He has super little ears and he watches one the whole time. Much as I like Goodwill, he can be rather aloof – though not nearly as aloof as Doublet. But he does have a nice face and a lovely pair of eyes and, when I clipped his head and neck out recently, he was very kind and gentlemanly about it.'

As it transpired, the gentlemanly Goodwill was the only horse Princess Anne took to Badminton – not to ride in the three-day event but to hack around Badminton Park as a continuation of his get-fit programme. Both Flame Gun and Arthur of Troy, her two prospective mounts for the Championships, had to be withdrawn shortly before the competition through minor training injuries.

Laureate II was also withdrawn, not because of injury but because Mark could ride only three horses. He'd had two sharply contrasted experiences with this potentially brilliant horse during the spring one-day events that preceded Badminton: at Ermington Laureate was eliminated for three refusals; at Liphook he won a

G

section of the Advanced from a high-class field.

If 1976 hadn't been Olympic year Laureate might have been taken to Badminton – and he might have won the title. But Mark was aware that the selectors might still not forgive his earlier lapses. A place on the Olympic team was his obvious goal at Badminton; the three horses he therefore chose to ride were Brazil, Favour and Persian Holiday – all of whom had a record sheet that was unbesmirched by eliminations.

He elected to ride Persian Holiday last ('as I thought he had the best chance of winning') but it proved an unfortunate decision. Only two of his horses' scores could count for the competition and the international Ground Jury decided that, like it or lump it, the last of his three mounts would have to be the one to go *hors concours*. In the dressage Persian Holiday was, in fact, the best of the trio and he would have been lying in fourth place. But the others had also performed creditably and Mark was lying equal fifth on Brazil and seventh on Favour when the two days of dressage were over.

It was the cross-country phase that finished Brazil's Olympic chances. 'He lost a shoe at the third fence,' said Mark, 'and from then on he was never really going well, probably because he was feeling his foot.' He still jumped boldly into the Badminton lake, but, with the water dragging against his legs and checking his momentum, he was floundering when he reached the next fence. This was a tree-trunk suspended over water; Brazil attempted to jump it but caught his forelegs on the fence and nosedived into the water beyond. Mark then lay on his back, with his legs in the air while water drained out of his boots, before continuing an unsatisfactory journey. It ended abruptly when Brazil refused twice at the Sunken Road (the twenty-third of thirty-five cross-country fences) and was retired.

The round left painful reminders in more ways than one, for Mark injured his knee when Brazil fell and he had a pretty tortured ride on his next mount, Favour, as a result. But the pain certainly didn't show in the performance. The eight-year-old grey mare displayed impressive scope and agility and cohesion; with a fast clear round she finished the day in third place.

Trials of the Badminton set

Royals, tweeds and shooting sticks. But the sport's the thing, writes Dennis Johnson

ONE OF THOSE strident English country lady voices, which never seem to be blown any fainter by the stern winds of Socialism, could be heard declaiming plain truths beside the collecting ring at Badminton horse trials yesterday. "Isn't it amazing," she demanded of her bowler-hatted partner, " that 25 years ago we were sitting on straw bales ?"

Amazing, certainly. Badminton, in its silver jubilee year, is a massive tribute to what a bit of steady Royal custom can achieve. The spectator stands would not disgrace Maine Road and the size of the car parks confirms the place of the three-

day trials in the nation's calendar of big sports happenings.

It's not just the horse trials though. Royal patronage means good business, and yesterday the acreage of sunny parkland devoted to trade stands was larger by far than the arena—a third of a mile of salesmen, in two ranks, forming a great processional way for the arriving crowds.

The first day of Badminton, as usual, was for dressage which, as the jubilee programme explained, is intended to promote "the harmonious development of the physique and ability of the horse." On the whole, the early crowds seemed to find this worthy object less "appealing than the prospect of

some alfresco shopping in the fine spring weather.

"Zacharias, water proofers, Oxford," had to be visited, "Cambrian Flyfishers," pot-shops, anorak shops, and shops displaying the finest in tweed fashion.

Still, the sport's the thing. The trick at Badminton is to ignore Royalty, which everyone does, in a quaintly considerate manner, stealing a glance only under the guise of being attracted by an interesting fetlock. It wasn't too hard to ignore them yesterday, because the main Royal Flush, as one official traitorously described it, was only just beginning to arrive to stay with the Duke of Beaufort at Badminton House. Princess Anne, unable to ride because two of her horses had, as they say, "gorn lame," drove past the press tent in her Range Rover,

giving the boys an enigmatic smile.

As one says, the sport's the thing. There is a record entry of 70 for the jubilee trials, from which will emerge the most likely riders to form the British Equestrian team for the Olympics at Montreal. Appropriately, for Badminton, the father of one of the competitors, Robert Desoudry, owns the land on which the Olympics will be held. There is also a record turnout of 230 British and European press and television representatives, including many who are there simply to ignore the appearance of Princess Margaret.

In spite of everything, the scents are still of creosote, hot tack and, just occasionally, dung.

"Hello, Fiona, my dear—how on earth have you all been?" The tone is a reassurance in a difficult world.

British Rail and Ministry head for row

By CHARLES COOK

Further differences of opinion between the British Railways Board and their masters in the Department of the Environment are likely to emerge shortly after the announcement yesterday that the board has commissioned its own study of the future prospects for the railways—despite the impending arrival of the Government's Green Paper on transport.

The British Rail study, which will be completed by June was

resignation of Sir Richard Marsh.

But comments from Ministers and officials within the Department have given some indication of the way they are thinking. Announcing the independent survey yesterday, Sir Richard referred obliquely to these comments as "a whole collection of cliches aimed at the semi-literate."

The differences between the two sides are exemplified by one statistic vital to the diffi-

Wife of pop star cleared on drugs

Krissie Wood, wife of Rolling Stones and Faces lead guitarist Ronnie Wood, and her friend Audrey Burgon were found not guilty at Kingston Crown Court yesterday of possessing cocaine.

The jury took four hours 40 minutes to reach the verdict. Afterwards, Mrs Wood (27) said: "I am glad I have been vindicated. I'm very happy to have been found innocent. I just want to go and have a nice baby." During the trial Mrs Wood disclosed she was pregnant.

In December last year Mrs Wood and Miss Burgon were cleared of a charge of possessing cannabis but the jury failed

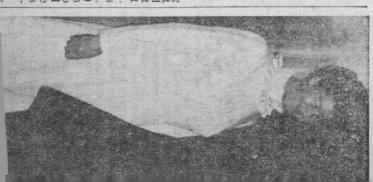

'She's a sweet mare,' said Mark, 'very friendly in the stable and rather fun to look after. But, to ride, she's a bit more temperamental and highly-strung – and very, very sensitive. The whole time I'm trying to calm her down, so that she relaxes and concentrates on the job in hand.' As could be seen by the selectors, congregated around the closed-circuit television screen in the directors' tent, the mare concentrated admirably on the Badminton cross-country.

Mark had a pain-killing injection into his injured knee before setting out to tackle the fifteen-and-a-half mile Badminton course for the third time. He had been first to go on Brazil and was last of the seventy starters on Persian Holiday. There were few people left around the steeplechase course and, except for the officials, the two sections of roads and tracks were (as usual) virtually deserted. Even the huge cross-country crowd had thinned out by the time Persian Holiday reached Phase D.

The big chestnut horse, with his elongated stride, was not being pushed and he jumped round well, except for a refusal at the fence in the lake where Brazil had fallen. Like Brazil, Persian Holiday reached the tree trunk on an awkward stride; Mark believes he could probably still have jumped it safely but, since he was running *hors concours*, it seemed an unnecessary risk. So he turned the horse back and gave him another run at it.

Meanwhile Lucinda Prior-Palmer had jumped with marvellous verve on her 'second-string', the ten-year-old Wide Awake, and she ended the day with a comfortable lead. Behind her, in a tight bunch, came Hugh Thomas on Playamar, Mark on Favour and Richard Meade on Jacob Jones.

When the leading contenders circled around the collecting ring the following afternoon, awaiting their turn in the show jumping, Princess Anne was there to wish them luck from the back of Goodwill. The horse tended to be upset by crowds and the collecting ring at Badminton seemed a good place to help him get used to them. 'I can remember standing with him at Burghley, waiting for the show jumping at the World Championships,' said the Princess. 'He'd been standing like the Rock of Gibraltar, half asleep and not bothering, until the applause started for the horse before him and he suddenly tensed up. Since then we've tried to have him in the atmosphere so that he gets used to it and doesn't worry about the clapping so much.'

There was plenty to clap about at Badminton and Goodwill still looked distinctly unhappy with each burst of applause, which followed clear rounds from the four leaders and left their final position unchanged. Then came the sad sequel. Lucinda Prior-Palmer had received the Whitbread Trophy from the Queen and just completed the lap of honour when Wide Awake collapsed and died in the arena. In the end, it was Princess Anne (with memories of a similar experience with Doublet) who chauffeured Lucinda away from the gathering crowd.

Her grief at the loss of a much-loved horse was to be made more painful by the abusive letters which followed her home. Having seen the *rapport* of horse and rider on the cross-country course; having seen their bubbling enthusiasm still intact when they jumped a clear round in the show jumping, it was impossible to believe that anybody could accuse Lucinda of blatant cruelty. Yet, in their awful ignorance, that is exactly what the letter writers did. There were even abusive letters to Frank Weldon, for building the cross-country course, and to Mark Phillips for riding round it.

Before the death of Wide Awake, we had all been marvelling at the great good fortune of Lucinda in having two horses of Olympic calibre. But Be Fair had always been her main hope for Montreal and, as was inevitable, both horse and rider were on the list of five Olympic 'probables' announced that week. The others were Princess Anne on Goodwill, Mark with both Favour and Persian Holiday, Hugh Thomas on Playamar and Richard Meade on Jacob Jones.

It was only ten days after Badminton that an obscure novice contest in Dorset produced more banner headlines. Princess Anne, riding Columbus's sister Candlewick in the Portman Horse Trials, was concussed in a fall, which (by all accounts) must rate as the most spine-chilling of the season. The mare hit the top of a fence, catapulted her rider on to rock-hard ground and then fell on top of her. Princess Anne was badly concussed and vividly bruised, but the much publicized hair-line fracture to the wing of a vertebrae was, fortunately, of little concern.

She has no recollection of the fall; indeed, for a while, she had no recollection of even travelling to Dorset to take part in the contest. Yet a few months later, while in training for the Olympics, she still made light of it. 'It wasn't too drastic,' she said. 'The doctors didn't seem to think I'd done myself too much damage – and it was muscle rather than bone damage. I was unconscious for about ten minutes and then I progressed steadily back to my present state of health.'

The hardness of the ground, a continuing problem for those preparing their horses for a possible trip to Montreal, also left its mark on Candlewick. 'She was sore and stiff after her fall,' said Alison Oliver, who trains the mare and thinks a great deal of her, 'so she was turned out at Hampton Court with Columbus.'

Princess Anne still didn't look too well during mid-May at Tidworth, where she and Mardi Gras were eliminated on the cross-country, but she seemed splendidly fit by the time of the Bramham Three-Day Event in early June. It was at the Yorkshire meeting that she and Goodwill, running *hors concours*, effectively swept aside any doubts concerning their well-being. They missed one circuit of the steeplechase course and three kilometres of roads and tracks but, far from reducing the fitness test for Princess Anne, this probably increased it since Goodwill, clearly delighted to be back in action, was still pulling like a train when he reached the cross-country.

'I didn't realize he was *that* fit,' said the Princess, as she gave an enthusiastic blow-by-blow account of her round to Alison Oliver – who, though no longer involved in Goodwill's training, was naturally watching her former charge with keen interest. It had been Goodwill at his bold and powerful best; there no longer seemed any shadow of a doubt that Princess Anne would be on the plane for Montreal.

15 | The Montreal Olympics

The final Olympic work-out took place on a blistering late June day at Osberton, against a backcloth of tinsel lake and softly curvaceous pasture. Despite dark rumours which suggested that some of the horses were not 100 per cent sound, there were no absentees among the 'probables'; all five riders were still in close contention for the four places on the Olympic team and there were heated arguments as to which of them would finally be left out and named as reserve.

The selectors must have had some preconceived ideas. 'As I see it,' said their Chairman, Lord Hugh Russell, before the Osberton cross-country began, 'there are two definites for the team, so we have three riders going for the other two places.' He naturally declined to say who the two 'definites' might be – and conjecture among the assembled Press was so divided as to be equally un-enlightening. The talents of the riders, balanced with the ability of their horses, meant that the five had quite remarkably level claims.

Osberton was to be a test of well-being rather than a trial of strength – or, as chef d'équipe Colonel Bill Lithgow put it, 'more like practising in the nets than the real thing'. But that didn't reduce its relevance. Mark was fully conscious of the need to prove Favour's well-being, especially since the mare had hit a front joint the previous week and had only been back in work for three days.

But, first to go on the stretch of the cross-country course that wasn't reached by the loudspeakers, he had to weave an uncomfortable path through those who were crossing his route and, as a result, the mare gave the second fence an almighty clout. Looking back at her hindlegs to see if any damage had been done, he was ill-prepared for the third fence and Favour stopped. So twenty penalties appeared on the scoreboard without many people appreciating that there were justifiable excuses. 'Considering that she was short of work, she really went very well indeed,' said Mark, 'and there has been no more trouble from her joint since then.' He had a good ride on Persian Holiday, with whom he came out best of the 'probables' – but since the selectors were more impressed with Favour's three-day event form, the results of his two mounts were the wrong way round.

There were no such problems for Princess Anne. Goodwill, looking like a coffee-table portrait of perfection, sailed round the cross-country, his well-being clearly visible in his gleaming coat and long, relaxed stride. 'Being on the short-list I consider to be an achievement,' said the Princess. 'If I get to Montreal I will consider that to be another achievement – and, if I actually get a ride, that will be quite something'.

And, of course, she did get a ride. The selectors went off in a whispering huddle after the Osberton work-out and finally cast their die. Princess Anne, Lucinda Prior-Palmer, Hugh Thomas and Richard Meade would be on the Olympic team; Mark would go to Montreal as reserve rider, taking both his horses.

'I wouldn't be natural if I wasn't disappointed,' said Mark, 'but it's still an honour to be selected to go as reserve.' The reserve position is by no means an easy one to fill but, according to Bill Lithgow, Mark filled this selfless role admirably – 'he was truly excellent and enormously helpful.'

The five riders went into training at Ascot the following week and – when photographers, journalists and broadcasters turned up to meet them a few days later – it was clear that they were already a happy and united team. There was no sign of tension. Laughter was much in evidence, as was easy camaraderie and an almost tangible delight in being free to do their own chosen thing.

'But it is fun,' said Lucinda, when someone commented on the absence of tension. 'I can't tell you how peaceful it is, with no telephone ringing and no bills to pay.'

'We do it because we enjoy it,' added Princess Anne.

The two girls were understandably shirty when someone asked daft questions about the death of Doublet: was Princess Anne upset when it happened? Did she worry about the same thing happening again? Lucinda sighed and looked heavenwards; Princess Anne said tartly, 'If you thought about that sort of thing you'd never get out of bed.' But it was no more than a momentary and superficial irritation, like pausing to swat a fly during a happy picnic.

Goodwill, Favour and Persian Holiday were among the horses that were loaded on to a plane at Gatwick at six o'clock in the morning on 13 July. The riders followed on a scheduled flight from Heathrow the same day; the fact that the Royal couple travelled economy-class with the rest of the team may have seemed newsworthy to the papers, but it was taken for granted by their companions. There were to be no special privileges. 'It has always been made terribly easy for us,' said Bill Lithgow. 'Her Royal Highness has never suggested being anything else but an ordinary team member – and neither have we.'

The team's final destination was Bromont, fifty miles from Montreal. It proved unexpectedly beautiful with its river and lush pasture and thickly wooded hills. 'It's much greener than England,' said the Princess, 'and the horses appreciate that.'

The Royal couple stayed in Windsor Place, in the heavily guarded equestrian Olympic Village. It was somewhat different from that other place, at Windsor in England, but they hadn't gone to Bromont looking for luxury and Princess Anne described the accommodation as 'excellent'.

The training facilities were also excellent; there were plenty of practice areas and mile upon mile of trails through wooded hills, where the horses built up stronger and harder muscles. Goodwill was positively – indeed almost literally – bursting with health and vitality when the Princess prepared him for his dressage test on the first day of the Olympic contest.

She is only too well aware of the horse's tendency to boil over in this phase. 'He has the ability to do a really super test,' she said. 'He won the Hickstead Combined Training Championship one year, which really rather amazed everyone – but it was his first

Princess Anne and Moriarty test the Osberton water before the final Olympic work-out . . . and Mark follows. *Below:* In training for Montreal (left to right): Lucinda Prior-Palmer on Be Fair, Princess Anne on Goodwill, Richard Meade on Jacob Jones, Hugh Thomas on Playamar and Mark Phillips on Favour.

The Royal couple leave for
Montreal. 'If I actually get
a ride,' said Princess Anne,
'that will be quite
something.' *Below:* The
Princess with her team–mate
Lucinda Prior-Palmer.

A last minute dusting before
the Olympic dressage.

Goodwill in the Olympic dressage and after his fall on the cross-country. 'I don't remember anything about it,' said the Princess, referring to that part of the course which she completed after her fall. The Queen watched from fence 2, looking like a portrayal of maternal concern.

test of the summer and he was much more relaxed than usual.'

Relaxation was rather more difficult in Bromont. The announcer had appealed to the crowds to keep absolutely quiet and the Princess rode in to an electric silence; 'I could hear things that I would never normally hear,' she said. Goodwill, fit to run for his life on cross-country day, found it all rather too intoxicating.

'He did some movements quite beautifully and there were some marvellous extensions,' said Claude Allhusen, who is on the British Horse Society's panel of dressage judges. 'The mistakes were just because he was bubbling over – especially at the end when we rather feared that he was going to jump into the judges' tent! But I certainly don't think he was generously marked; if anything I think the judges were rather harsh on him.'

The Allhusens were remembering their own horse, Laurieston, competing in the Munich Olympics with Richard Meade four years earlier. He, too, had marred a performance that was full of impulsion and vitality by bubbling over – but they had been pleasantly surprised by the judges' leniency. 'We were hoping it would be the same for Princess Anne,' said Claude.

But it wasn't. Goodwill's 91.25 penalties were to leave the Princess in twenty-sixth place at the end of the dressage – 45 points behind the West German leader, Karl Schultz on Madrigal. This was a disappointment but not a disaster. The other British riders were better placed: Lucinda and Be Fair, with a lovely light and rhythmic test, were fifth with 62.91 penalties; Richard was twelfth on Jacob Jones (73.75) and Hugh was sixteenth on Playamar (85). Everyone was hoping that they would all improve their positions in the speed, endurance and cross-country phase.

The soft wet sand on the steeplechase course was to emphasize the endurance aspect of the test; so, too, were the steep gradients on the cross-country. The fences were not considered difficult, but the twists and turns between them meant that it would be virtually impossible to maintain an easy rhythmic stride.

It was to prove an agonizing day for the British supporters. Hugh Thomas, charting the course for his team, had a fall at the lake (fence 22) and Playamar finished very lame; Princess Anne fell at the nineteenth; Richard Meade then relieved the gloom with a good clear round on Jacob Jones, but it returned with the depressing news that Lucinda Prior-Palmer's exuberant clear on Be Fair had ended with another British horse on the injured list. The little chestnut had slipped a tendon off his hock and, with the memories of a similar disaster still all too easily recaptured, Mark recognized it instantly. 'He's done exactly the same as Columbus,' he said, as Lucinda rode through the finish.

Princess Anne, second to go for the British team, had set off with splendid confidence. The Queen was beside the second fence, looking like a portrayal of maternal concern as her daughter and her horse went safely past. Bertie Hill, one of four trainers who had been helping the team in Montreal and the one to whom Princess Anne had looked for assistance, was beside the group of fences numbered fourteen to sixteen – and he was delighted to see her going so well. He was equally pleased when she returned from the loop which took her over the seventeenth fence and proceeded to sail over the eighteenth; he was then appalled by the sight of Goodwill turning upside-down.

The horse had hit a soft patch of ground a few strides out, which checked his momentum; he had also slid on take-off and his hind legs were crossed as he hit the zigzag rails over a ditch. Princess Anne lay dazed and mildly concussed as Bertie sprinted towards her. He was not, he decided on arrival, in the least bit anxious for her to continue – but Her Royal Highness (despite her thoughts about 'carrying sport too far') had clearly set out on a do-or-die course. 'I see no reason why I shouldn't go on now,' she told those who had been kneeling beside her and, when she saw the reluctant Bertie Hill, she said: 'I'm off – so give me a leg up.' But she remembers neither her words nor the remaining seventeen fences which Goodwill jumped so immaculately.

The Princess hadn't been worried by the nineteenth ('the trouble was that I wasn't worried enough!') and the rest of the British contingent hadn't been much bothered either – until it became evident that the right-hand approach, softened by rain overnight and still further by another downpour while the contest was in progress, had become distinctly boggy.

Diana Mason, who was to ride for Britain in the Olympic

dressage, was anxious to send a message to that effect back to the start but the boy on the bicycle, who was due to collect such information, had failed to arrive because his chain kept falling off; and the supporter, to whom it was eventually given, couldn't get through the tight security. It sounded a little like *Dad's Army*: Captain Mainwaring sending a boy on a man's errand on a clapped-out bike. But all twelve teams, barred from using walkie-talkies and attempting to relay messages from thirty-six fences in the middle of sodden fields, were forced to use similar methods. It normally works wonderfully well, but this was yet another sign that luck had abandoned the British.

Had the message arrived before the Princess set out, Bill Lithgow would have alerted her to the problems concerning the right-hand side of the fence, and it might have made a vital difference to the individual scores. But the British team was already out of the contest because of two lame horses.

On paper the team was lying second to the United States and the injured Be Fair was fourth, just under ten points ahead of Richard Meade who eventually finished in that position on Jacob Jones. Princess Anne flew the flag by reappearing for the final phase and jumping a slow clear round that left her in twenty-fourth place; Karl Schultz, the overnight leader, dropped back to third when Madrigal made two mistakes.

So the United States riders, a marvellously skilled and stylish quartet, won not only the team gold medal, but also the individual gold and silver through Tad Coffin on Bally Cor and Michael Plumb on Better and Better.

It was, of course, a disappointing end for the British riders–but they all accepted their misfortunes with smiling good grace and remained a united team. This wasn't the end of the road for any of them. The Royal couple continue to nurture their seasoned campaigners and patiently school their novices; both could be involved in another Olympic contest in 1980. When asked about her own ambitions for the next Olympic Games, Princess Anne gave a simple and practical answer: 'It all depends on whether I find another horse with as much ability as Goodwill.'

Appendix I : The event horses ridden by Princess Anne and Mark Phillips

ARTHUR OF TROY (1967), bay gelding, 16.2 h.h., sire: Raisin, dam: Rosetime. Owned and ridden by Princess Anne to finish fifth in his first three-day event at Bramham in 1974 and second in the Midland Bank Novice Championship later that year. In 1975 he finished tenth in the Ledyard Farm Three-Day Event (USA).

BRAZIL (1967), brown gelding, 17.2 h.h., sire: Tiopoletto, dam: Almond. Owned by Mrs R. Boucher and first ridden by John Smart with whom he completed Tidworth, Punchestown (Ireland) and Boekelo (Holland). Partnered by Mark at Burghley in 1975 to finish sixteenth, but retired during the cross-country at Badminton in 1976.

CANDLEWICK (1969), brown mare, 17 h.h., sire: Night Watch, dam: Trim Ann. A half-sister to Columbus, owned by HM the Queen and ridden by Princess Anne. Began competing in novice one-day events in the autumn of 1975.

CASETTE (1970), chestnut gelding, 16.2 h.h., sire: Marine Corps. Owned and ridden by Mark, he began novice one-day events in the spring of 1976 when he won a class at Wramplingham in Norfolk first time out.

CHICAGO III (1962), grey gelding, 16.1½ h.h., sire: Prickly, dam: Bella. Owned by Bertie Hill, with whom he won Advanced Classes at Wylye and Chatsworth in 1969. Ridden by Mark in the winning British team for the 1970 World Championships, where he was eleventh individually. Subsequently sold to Germany.

COLUMBUS (1965), grey gelding, 17 h.h., sire: Colonist II, dam: Trim Ann. Owned by HM the Queen and first ridden by Princess Anne, with whom he won an Intermediate Class at Liphook in 1972. Ridden by Mark from 1973 onwards. Won Badminton in 1974 and was leading individually in the World Championships at Burghley later that year until withdrawn with a hock injury on the morning of the final show jumping phase. Hopes that he might be back in action before the Montreal Olympics were thwarted when the hock trouble recurred at the beginning of 1976.

DOUBLET (1963), chestnut gelding, 16.2 h.h., sire: Doubtless, dam: Swate. Owned and bred by HM the Queen and subsequently given to Princess Anne, who rode him into fifth place at her first Badminton in 1971. She won the individual title in the European Championships with him later that year, but leg trouble kept him out of contention for a place on the 1972 Olympic team. Sustained a broken leg while being exercised in the spring of 1974 and had to be put down.

DRUMWHILL (1970), bay gelding, 17 h.h., sire: Shelley's Boy. Owned and ridden by Mark, with whom he started novice one-day events in 1976, winning at Wellesbourne.

FAVOUR (1968), grey mare, 16.3 h.h., sire: Hardraw Scar, dam: Grace. Owned by Mrs Carpendale, who gave Mark a half share in her at the beginning of 1976. Ridden into second place by Mark at Tidworth in 1975, and into fourth place by John Kersley at Burghley that autumn. Reunited with Mark, the mare finished third in the 1976 Badminton and was later chosen as one of the reserve horses for the Olympic Games.

FLAME GUN (1967), chestnut gelding, 16.1 h.h., sire: Vulgan, dam: Hope. A son of the former Irish international three-day event mare, he is owned and ridden by Princess Anne with whom he finished second at Tidworth in 1974. Was due to contest his first Badminton in 1976 until a minor injury in training forced his withdrawal.

GOODWILL (1965), brown gelding, 16.2 h.h., sire: Evening Trial, dam: Mrs Connor. Brought out as a show jumper by Alison Dawes, he was an immensely promising novice but a disappointment when he reached Grade A. Later bought by HM the Queen and ridden by Princess Anne to become a very consistent three-day event horse. He was eighth at Badminton in 1973, but fell at fence 2 in Kiev where Princess Anne was defending her European title. Subsequently fourth at Badminton in 1974, twelfth in the World Championships at Burghley the same year and second in the European Championships at Luhmühlen in 1975 when competing for the British team. Selected for the British Olympic team in Montreal, where he had an unlucky cross-country fall but completed the course.

GREAT OVATION (1962), brown gelding, 16.3½ h.h., sire: Three Cheers, dam: Cyprus Valence. Owned by Miss Flavia Phillips and Mark, he won Badminton twice, in 1971 and 1972. Mark also rode him in the British teams that won the European Championship in 1971 (where he was sixth individually) and the gold medal at the 1972 Olympic Games in Munich. Retired from eventing at the end of 1974.

GRETNA GREEN (1968), black mare, 16.3 h.h., sire: Highland Flight, dam: Molly Mareless. Owned and normally ridden by Janet Hodgson, with whom she won a section of the Advanced Two-Day Event at Osberton in 1975. Mark was asked to partner the mare at Burghley later that year (when Janet was suffering from concussion) and he rode her into second place.

KOOKABURRA (1958), liver chestnut gelding, sire: Renwood. Owned by Miss Flavia Phillips and lent to Mark, who rode him in the Pony Club Horse Trials Championships and then in novice one-day events. Won two novices, but lacked the scope to go any further and was subsequently given to Mark's sister, Sarah, as a hunter. Put down in 1974 because of severe arthritis.

LAUREATE II (1966), bay gelding, 17 h.h., sire: Scottish Venture, dam: Queen's Laurel. Owned by Mr and Mrs T. R. Mills and ridden by Mark. Won his first three-day events at Tidworth and Wylye in 1973, and finished a close second at Boekelo in Holland at the end of the same year. Later developed leg trouble and, in the summer of 1975, the habit of getting his tongue over the bit. Came back to win the Advanced Class at Liphook in 1976 but was withdrawn from Badminton, where Mark had three other horses to ride.

MAID MARION (1965), bay mare, 16.2 h.h., sire: Suki de Su, dam: Rosebud. Owned by Bertie and Tony Hill, and ridden by Tony to finish second in the Junior European Championships at Eridge in 1972. Ridden by Mark to win the 1973 Burghley Horse Trials. Subsequently retired to stud.

MARDI GRAS (1969), chestnut gelding, 16.1 h.h., sire: Manicou, dam: Easter. Owned and ridden by Princess Anne, with whom he finished third in a novice section of the Bramham three-day event in 1975. Eliminated at a water jump at Tidworth the following spring.

PERSIAN HOLIDAY (1967), chestnut gelding, 17 h.h., sire: Blue Shah, dam: Bank Holiday IV. Owned and ridden by Mark, he won Tidworth in 1974 during his second year in eventing. Was placed in all thirteen of the events he contested during 1973 and 1974. Developed tendon trouble in 1975 and underwent an operation. Ran *hors concours* at Badminton in 1976 and was later chosen as one of the reserve horses for the Olympic Games.

PURPLE STAR (1961), bay gelding, 15.3 h.h., sire: Flush Royal, dam: Stella. Owned by Colonel Sir John Miller and ridden by

Princess Anne to whom he was subsequently given. The talented son of a former Olympic three-day-event mare, he gave Princess Anne her first taste of eventing. Later began refusing and was retired to the hunting field in 1970.

ROCK ON (1960), bay gelding, 16.1 h.h., sire: Black Rock. Owned and ridden by Mark, with whom he finished fourth at Burghley in 1967 and at Badminton in 1968. Was short-listed for the 1968 Olympic Games, but broke down on the day before the final trial. Seventh in the 1969 European Championships. Died in 1972 after a tendon operation.

ROYAL OCEAN (1961), brown gelding, 16 h.h., sire: Guersant, dam: Santa Baby. Qualified for the first Midland Bank Novice Championship in 1969 by winning at Windsor, but retired on the cross-country course. Retired from eventing shortly afterwards.

Appendix II : Records

OLYMPIC GAMES

Mexico, 1968

TEAM: 1. Great Britain (Major Derek Allhusen on Lochinvar, Jane Bullen on Our Nobby, Richard Meade on Cornishman V and Ben Jones on The Poacher)
2. USA
3. Australia

INDIVIDUAL: 1. Jean-Jacques Guyon (France) on Pitou
2. Major Derek Allhusen (GB) on Lochinvar
3. Michael Page (USA) on Foster

Munich, 1972

TEAM: 1. Great Britain (Mary Gordon-Watson on Cornishman V, Bridget Parker on Cornish Gold, Richard Meade on Laurieston and Mark Phillips on Great Ovation)
2. USA
3. West Germany

INDIVIDUAL: 1. Richard Meade (GB) on Laurieston
2. Alessa Argenton (Italy) on Woodland
3. Jan Jonsson (Sweden) on Sarajevo

H

Montreal, 1976

TEAM: 1. USA (Tad Coffin on Bally Cor, Michael Plumb on Better and Better, Bruce Davidson on Irish Cap and Mary Anne Tauskey on Marcus Aurelius)
2. West Germany
3. Australia

INDIVIDUAL: 1. Tad Coffin (USA) on Bally Cor
2. Michael Plumb (USA) on Better and Better
3. Karl Schultz (West Germany) on Madrigal

WORLD CHAMPIONSHIPS

Punchestown, 1970

TEAM: 1. Great Britain (Mary Gordon-Watson on Cornishman V, Richard Meade on The Poacher, Mark Phillips on Chicago III and Stewart Stevens on Benson)
2. France

Only two teams finished

INDIVIDUAL: 1. Mary Gordon-Watson (GB) on Cornishman V
2. Richard Meade (GB) on The Poacher
3. James Wofford (USA) on Kilkenny
(Mark Phillips finished eleventh on Chicago III)

Burghley, 1974

TEAM: 1. USA (Bruce Davidson on Irish Cap, Michael Plumb on Good Mixture, Denny Emerson on Victor Dakin and Don Sachey on Plain Sailing)
2. Great Britain
3. West Germany

INDIVIDUAL: 1. Bruce Davidson (USA) on Irish Cap
2. Michael Plumb (USA) on Good Mixture
3. Hugh Thomas (GB) on Playamar
(Columbus, ridden by Mark Phillips, was leading until a hock injury caused his withdrawal prior to the final show jumping. Princess Anne finished twelfth on Goodwill)

EUROPEAN CHAMPIONSHIPS

Haras du Pin, 1969

TEAM: 1. Great Britain (Richard Walker on Pasha, Major Derek Allhusen on Lochinvar, Pollyann Hely-Hutchinson on Count Jasper and Ben Jones on The Poacher)
2. USSR
3. West Germany

INDIVIDUAL: 1. Mary Gordon-Watson (GB) on Cornishman V
2. Richard Walker (GB) on Pasha
3. Bernd Messman (W. Germany) on Windspiel
(Mark Phillips finished seventh on Rock On)

Burghley, 1971

TEAM: 1. Great Britain (Mary Gordon-Watson on Cornishman V, Debbie West on Baccarat, Mark Phillips on Great Ovation and Richard Meade on The Poacher)
2. USSR
3. Ireland

INDIVIDUAL: HRH Princess Anne (GB) on Doublet
2. Debbie West (GB) on Baccarat
3. Stewart Stevens (GB) on Classic Chips
(Mark Phillips finished sixth on Great Ovation)

Kiev, 1973

TEAM: 1. West Germany (Kurt Mergler on Vaibel, Herbert Blöcker on Albrant, Harry Klugmann on El Paso and Horst Karsten on Sioux)
2. USSR
3. Great Britain

INDIVIDUAL: 1. Alexander Evdokimov (USSR) on Jeger
2. Herbert Blöcker (W. Germany) on Albrant
3. Horst Karsten (W. Germany) on Sioux

Luhmühlen, 1975

TEAM: 1. USSR (Peter Gornuschko on Gusar, Viktor Kalinin on Araks, Vladimir Lanügin on Reflex and Vladimir Tischkin on Flot)
2. Great Britain
3. West Germany

INDIVIDUAL: 1. Lucinda Prior-Palmer (GB) on Be Fair
2. HRH Princess Anne (GB) on Goodwill
3. Peter Gornuschko (USSR) on Gusar

BADMINTON THREE-DAY EVENT

1968 Jane Bullen on Our Nobby
1969 Richard Walker on Pasha
1970 Richard Meade on The Poacher
1971 Mark Phillips on Great Ovation
1972 Mark Phillips on Great Ovation
1973 Lucinda Prior-Palmer on Be Fair
1974 Mark Phillips on Columbus
1975 (Cancelled)
1976 Lucinda Prior-Palmer on Wide Awake

Glossary

Badminton: Established in 1949 by the Duke of Beaufort and held on his Gloucestershire estate, the Badminton Horse Trials constitute the oldest established three-day event in the world. The selectors use Badminton form as a guide-line when choosing horses and riders for international three-day-event teams.

Box, The: An enclosure where riders weigh out at the start of the speed, endurance and cross-country phase, and weigh in at the finish. The box is also used for the ten-minute compulsory halt before the cross-country, during which time the horses are examined by two judges and a vet.

Broken down: Term used to describe a horse that has badly strained or ruptured the back tendon in one of its legs.

Burghley: Established in 1961 on the Marquess of Exeter's estate adjoining the Lincolnshire town of Stamford, the Burghley Horse Trials are now the major event of the autumn season in Britain. Two World Championships (1966 and 1974) and one European Championship (1971) have been staged there.

Coffin: A combination of cross-country fences, first used at Badminton. It comprises two fences with a ditch between them.

Combined Training Committee: Body responsible for administering the sport in Britain and for selecting international teams.

Dressage: A series of movements designed to test the horse's obedience and state of training, and the rider's ability to apply the aids correctly. Each movement is marked individually by the three judges; points are also given for the overall impression. The three judges' marks are then averaged and deducted from the maximum possible total to give a penalty score. This score is multiplied by the 'multiplying factor' (*q.v.*) to give the actual number of penalty points that the horse will carry through to the next phase.

Elephant Trap: A cross-country fence, often used at Badminton, which comprises sloping rails over a ditch.

Examination of horses: All horses undergo a veterinary inspection before the start of a three-day event. They are inspected again before the cross-country, and lastly on the morning of the final show jumping phase.

Fédération Equestre Internationale (FEI): The world ruling body for all equestrian sports except racing. Prince Philip has been the Federation's President since 1966.

Grading: There are three grades for event horses in Britain: I (Advanced), II (Intermediate) and III (Novice). Horses are upgraded through points gained at official horse trials.

Hobdayed: A horse that has undergone an operation for its wind.

Horse trials: A general term covering all eventing competitions, as does the description 'combined training'. The latter also covers contests in which only two of the three phases (usually dressage and show jumping) are included.

Hunter trials: Cross-country competitions, usually judged on a combination of faults and time.

Multiplying factor: The means by which the dressage phase of a three-day event can be made to exert 'the correct influence on the whole competition'. It varies between 1 and $2\frac{1}{2}$ according to the severity of the speed, endurance and cross-country (*q.v.*) and, to a lesser extent, of the show jumping (*q.v.*).

Nappy: Term used to describe a horse that disobeys its rider's instructions. Common examples of napping are refusing to enter a show jumping ring or to leave the company of other horses.

Normandy Bank: A cross-country fence first used for the 1969 European Championships at Haras du Pin, and since copied at Badminton and other venues. It requires the horse to jump on to a sleeper-faced bank and over a fence at the top from which there is a big drop to ground level.

One-day event: A contracted form of three-day eventing in which dressage, cross-country and show jumping are performed on the same day.

Penalty zone: An area surrounding steeplechase and cross-country fences. It extends ten metres before and twenty metres beyond each fence, at a width of ten metres from the boundary flags at each side. Falls outside the penalty zone are not penalized except by loss of time.

Refusal: A horse is said to have refused when it stops in front of a fence, and to have 'run out' when it swerves past the obstacle. Both forms of disobedience are penalized the same way.

Roads and tracks: These constitute the endurance aspect of a three-day event. There are two sections of roads and tracks to be covered during the speed, endurance and cross-country phase (*q.v.*).

Scoring: Penalty points are cumulative and the horse with the lowest number of penalties at the end of the final phase is the winner. In the case of equality, the horse with the faster cross-country round is awarded the higher place. See dressage, also speed, endurance and cross-country, and show jumping for methods of scoring for each phase.

Show jumping: The competition on the last day of a three-day event is not a severe test of the horse's jumping ability. Its object is to prove that, on the day after a severe test of endurance, the horse is still able to continue in service. Show jumping penalties in an international three-day event are incurred as follows:

Fence knocked down: 10 penalties

One or more feet in the water or on the landing tape: 10 penalties

Refusals (including running-out or circling): first: 10 penalties; second: 20 penalties; third: elimination

Fall of horse and/or rider: 30 penalties

Each second over the time allowed: $\frac{1}{4}$ penalty

Exceeding the time limit or taking the wrong course: elimination

Speed, endurance and cross-country: A test consisting of four separate sections: (1) and (3) roads and tracks, (2) steeplechase and (4) cross-country. The length of each section varies according to the importance of the competition, with a maximum total distance of 32.3 km (about 20 miles) for the Olympic Games and World Championships.

Time penalties can be incurred on all four sections of the course, though it is rare for anyone to exceed the 'optimum time' on the roads and tracks. For each second over the 'optimum time' competitors incur 0.8 of a penalty on the steeplechase and 0.4 on the cross-country.

Jumping penalties on the steeplechase and cross-country courses are incurred as follows:

Refusals (including running-out or circling): first: 20 penalties; second (at the same obstacle): 40 penalties; third (at the same obstacle): elimination

Fall of horse and/or rider: 60 penalties

Second fall of horse and/or rider on the steeplechase course: elimination

Third fall of horse and/or rider on the cross-country course: elimination

Taking the wrong course: elimination

Team competitions: The Olympic Games and the World and Continental Championships offer team as well as individual awards. Each team comprises four riders, but only the best three scores count towards the team total.

Three-day event: The name given to the full-scale test which covers dressage, then speed, endurance and cross-country and finally show jumping. An international contest is known as a *Concours Complet International*.

Tidworth: The venue for the Army Horse Trials, inaugurated as a one-day event in 1958 and extended to a three-day event in 1960, with the intention of giving inexperienced horses a relatively easy introduction to the three-day test.

Trout Hatchery: A feature of the cross-country course at Burghley (*q.v.*), which incorporates jumps into and out of water.

Weights: There is no weight restriction for the dressage phase, but in the speed, endurance and cross-country and the show jumping horses are required to carry a minimum of 75 kg.

Acknowledgements

Permission to use copyright photographs is acknowledged as follows, in order of appearance in the book:

Between pages 24 and 25 – black and white

Mark on Longdon Beauty – Mr Peter Phillips
Princess Anne – Camera Press
Pickles – Photonews
Pirate – Bucks Advertiser
Princess Anne at a polo match – John Scott
HM the Queen with Princess Anne – Camera Press
Prince Charles and Princess Anne – Camera Press
Kookaburra – Cyril Diamond
Purple Star – John Scott
Rock On at Haras du Pin (2) – E. D. Lacey
Chicago – E. D. Lacey
Winning British team – E. D. Lacey
Princess Anne with Alison Oliver – Camera Press
Alison Oliver – Camera Press
Doublet – Jim Meads
Great Ovation – E. D. Lacey
Royal Ocean – John Scott

Between pages 56 and 57 – colour

Doublet – John Scott
Great Ovation – Jim Meads
HM the Queen presenting rosette to Mark – John Scott
Princess Anne with Henry Cooper – E. D. Lacey
Mark with Richard Meade and Bridget Parker – E. D. Lacey
Goodwill in Dressage and Showjumping – E. D. Lacey

Trainers and Riders – Reginald Davis
Brazil – E. D. Lacey
Mardi Gras – Akhtar Hussein/Photographers International
Princess Anne portrait – John Scott
Princess Anne and Mark – Akhtar Hussein/Photographers
  International

Between pages 88 and 89 – black and white

Princess Anne at Eridge – Camera Press
Doublet at Eridge (2) – Camera Press
Goodwill at Kiev (2) – Leslie Lane
Arthur of Troy – Camera Press
Goodwill at Badminton – E. D. Lacey
Engagement photograph – Camera Press
Persian Holiday – Leslie Lane
Laureate – Camera Press
Columbus falls into water – E. D. Lacey
Columbus falls again – Camera Press
Columbus wins Badminton 1974 – Jim Meads
Columbus in World Championships – Jim Meads
Lucinda Prior-Palmer – Findlay Davidson
Janet Hodgson – Findlay Davidson
Winning US team – Leslie Lane

Between pages 104 and 105 – black and white

Princess Anne and Mark at Osberton (2) – Camera Press
British Olympic team – Press Association
Leaving for Montreal – Press Association
Princess Anne and Lucinda Prior-Palmer – Press Association
Before the dressage – Keystone Press Agency
Goodwill in the dressage – Leslie Lane
Goodwill in the cross-country – Leslie Lane
HM the Queen – Associated Press

Index

Compiled by Gordon Robinson

Albrant, 115
Alexandra, Princess, 57
Allhusen, The Hon. Mrs Claude, 105
Allhusen, Major Derek, 19, 21, 28, 30,
      33, 56, 89, 105, 113, 115
Almond, 109
Amberley Horse Show, 61, 62
Araks, 116
Archer, 12, 13
Argenton, Alessa, 113
Arthur of Troy, 87, 95, 97, 108
Ascot, 48, 103

Baccarat, 46, 52, 53, 58, 69, 115
Badminton, 34, 117, 118, 119
   Horse Trials, 11, 13, 16, 18, 49;
      1968: 20–1, 24, 29, 112, 116; **1969**:
      30, 33, 116; **1970**: 39, 116; **1971**:
      42–6, 50, 109, 110, 116; **1972**: 54,
      55, 56–7, 110, 116; **1973**: 61, 64–6,
      110, 116; **1974**: 75, 77–9, 83, 109,
      110, 116; **1975**: 86–7; **1976**:
      96–100, 108, 109, 110, 111, 116
Ballinkeele, 22
Bally Cor, 107, 114
Balmoral, 11, 48
Bandit, 11–12
Bank Holiday IV, 111
Banks, Trevor, 62, 63
Barberry, 22, 28
Be Fair, 66, 69, 88, 92, 100, 105, 106,
      107, 116
Beaufort, The Duke of, 117
Beaufort Pony Club, 12, 13, 19, 21, 65
Bella, 108
Ben Wyvis, 87, 92
Benenden, 14
Benson, 40
Better and Better, 107, 114

Biddlecombe, Terry, 15
Biddlecombe, Walter, 15, 16
Black Rock, 15, 112
Blöcker, Herbert, 115
Blue Shah, 111
Blue Star, 23
Boekelo three-day event: **1973**: 73–4,
      108, 111
Boucher, Mrs R., 108
Bradley, Caroline, 89
Bramham three-day event: **1974**: 108;
      1975: 93, 111; **1976**: 101
Brazil, 92–3, 95, 98, 99, 108
British Horse Society, 105
Bromont, 104–5
Bullen, Jane (now Mrs Holderness-
      Roddam), 14, 19, 21, 27, 28, 30,
      113, 116
Bullen, Jennie (now Mrs Loriston-
      Clarke), 12, 14
Bullen, Sarah, 27
Burghley, 13, 117, 121
   Horse Trials: **1967**: 18–19, 20, 110;
      1968: 28; **1972**: 59–60; **1973**: 68, 79,
      111; **1975**: 92–3, 108, 109, 110
   European Championships: **1971**: 47,
      49–54, 109, 110, 115, 117
   World Championships: **1966**: 117;
      1974: 80–4, 99, 109, 110, 114,
      117
Burghley House, 81

Candlewick, 100–1, 108
Carawich, 93
Carpendale, Mrs, 109
Casette, 108
Charles, HRH The Prince of Wales 9, 11,
      24
Chatsworth Horse Trials: **1969**: 36, 107

Chicago III, 39–41, 42, 108–9, 114
Cirencester Park, 61
Classic Chips, 52, 115
Coffin, Tad, 107, 114
Collins, Chris, 81
Colonist II, 57, 109
Columbus, 32, 49, 57, 59, 60, 62, 64–5,
    75, 77, 78, 81–4, 96, 100, 101, 106,
    108, 109, 114, 116
Connor, Mrs, 110
Cornish Gold, 58, 81, 113
Cornishman V, 17, 28, 30, 33, 40, 41,
    43, 45, 46, 53, 58, 113, 114, 115
Count Jasper, 33, 115
Crookham Horse Trials, 17
Cyprus Valence, 42, 110

Davidson, Bruce, 78, 83, 84, 87, 114
Dawes, Alison, 63, 110
Deurne three-day event, 42–3
Devon Loch, 83
Doublet, 34–6, 43–4, 45–6, 48–52, 54,
    57, 60, 66, 67–8, 75, 76, 77, 78,
    79, 80, 83, 97, 100, 104, 109, 115
Doubtless II, 34, 109
Drumwhill, 109

East Grinstead, 48
Easter, 111
El Paso, 115
Elizabeth, HM The Queen Mother, 83
Elizabeth II, HM The Queen 10, 11,
    12, 27, 34, 36, 57, 60, 61, 83, 96,
    100, 106, 108, 109, 110
Emerson, Denny, 114
Eridge, 27
    Horse Trials, 42, 47, 48, 58
    Junior European Championships:
    1972: 111
Ermington one-day event: 1976: 97
European Championships
    Haras du Pin: 1969: 30–3, 40, 41,
    110, 115, 119
    Burghley: 1971: 47, 49–54, 109, 110,
    115, 117
    Kiev: 1973: 66, 67–72, 110, 115
    Luhmühlen: 1975: 70, 87–92, 110, 116
Evdokimov, Alexander, 72
Evening Trial, 63, 110
Everdon one-day event, 15
Exeter, The Marquess of, 117

Fair and Square, 27, 28
Favour, 96, 98–9, 100, 102–3, 104, 109
Fédération Equestre Internationale
    (FEI), 118
Flame Gun, 61, 80, 95, 97, 109–10
Flot, 116
Flush Royal, 111
Foster, 113
Foxdor, 21, 28

Gambit, 36
Garth Pony Club, 11
Gatwick, 104
Geekie, Carolan, 88
Golden Griffin, 87
Good Mixture, 83, 114
Goodwill, 49, 62–6, 67, 68, 70, 73–4,
    75, 76, 77, 78, 81, 83–4, 86, 88,
    90–2, 95, 96, 97, 99–100, 101, 103,
    104, 105, 106, 107, 110, 114, 116
Gordon-Watson, Mary, 17, 28, 33, 40,
    41, 45, 53, 58, 59, 113, 114, 115
Gornuschko, Peter, 116
Grace, 109
Grand National: 1956: 83
Great Ovation, 34, 42–6, 48–9, 50, 52,
    53, 55, 56, 58, 59, 62, 64, 75, 77,
    78, 113, 115, 116
Great Somerford, 12, 13, 15, 45
Greensleeves, 11
Gretna Green, 87, 92–3, 110
Guersant, 112
Gusar, 116
Guyon, Jean-Jacques, 113

Hampton Court, 96, 101
Haras du Pin
    European Championships: 1969: 31–3,
    40, 41, 112, 115, 119
Hardraw Scar, 109
Harley, 87, 88, 91, 92
Hatherly, Sue, 87, 88, 92
Hawley, 34
Heathrow, 104
Hely-Hutchinson, Pollyann, 27, 33, 115
Hickstead Combined Training
    Championship, 105
High Jinks, 12–13, 14
Highland Flight, 110
Hill, Bertie, 16, 18, 21, 23, 39, 42, 43,
    68, 77, 106, 108, 111

Hill, Tony, 68, 111
Hodgson, Janet, 60, 69, 70, 71, 78, 87, 88, 90, 93, 110
Holyport, near Maidenhead, 9
Hope, 109–10
Howard, Lady Sarah Fitzalan, 12

Irish Cap, 78, 83, 114

Jacob Jones, 99, 100, 105, 106, 107
Jones, Staff-Sergeant Ben, 21, 28, 29, 30, 33, 113, 115
Jonsson, Jan, 113
Junior European Show Jumping Championships: 1959: 12

Kalinin, Viktor, 116
Karsten, Horst, 115
Kersley, John, 109
Kiev European Championships: 1973: 66, 67–72, 110, 115
Kilkenny, 114
Kinlet one-day event, 36
Klugmann, Harry, 115
Kookaburra, 13, 15, 16, 110–11

Lanügin, Vladimir, 116
Larkspur, 60, 69, 78, 88, 90
Laureate, 89
Laureate II, 73, 78–9, 86, 87, 89, 95, 97–8, 111
Laurieston, 56, 58, 59, 89, 105, 113
Ledbury Pony Club, 11, 12
Ledyard Farm (USA) three-day event: 1975: 87, 108
Liphook Horse Trials: 1967: 17; 1971: 43; 1972: 109; 1974: 32–3, 75–6; 1976: 98, 111
Lithgow, Colonel Bill, 18, 90, 102, 103, 104, 107
Lochinvar, 19, 21, 28, 29, 30, 33, 113, 115
Longdon Beauty, 10
Luhmühlen European Championships: 1975: 70, 87–92, 110, 116
Lüneburg, 89

Madrigal, 105, 107, 114
Maid Marion, 68, 79, 111
Manicou, 93, 111
Marcus Aurelius, 114
Mardi Gras, 54, 93, 101, 111

Marine Corps, 108
Marlborough, 14
Mason, Diana, 106–7
Meade, Richard, 21, 22, 28, 29, 30, 33, 39, 40, 41, 53, 56, 59, 69, 73, 76, 81, 89, 99, 100, 103, 105–6, 107, 113, 114, 115, 116
Mergler, Kurt, 115
Messman, Bernd, 115
Mexico Olympics: 1968: 28–30, 113
Midland Bank Novice Championship: 1969: 35–6, 112; 1974: 108
Miller, Colonel Sir John, 23, 26, 111
Mills, Mr and Mrs T. R., 111
Mixbury one-day event, 15
Moat House Riding School, 14
Molly Mareless, 110
Montreal Olympics: 1976: 100–7, 109, 110, 111, 114
Munich Olympics: 1972: 53, 54, 56–9, 105, 110, 113

Nicholas Nickleby, 22
Night Watch, 108
Norfolk, Lavinia Duchess of, 93
Norfolk, The Duke of, 12

Oliver, Alan, 45, 62–3
Oliver, Alison, 20, 23, 24–5, 34–5, 36, 44, 45, 47, 49, 54, 57, 60, 61, 62–3, 64, 75, 77, 79, 96, 101
Olivia, 80
Olympic Games
    Rome: 1960: 88
    Mexico: 1968: 28–30, 113
    Munich: 1972: 53, 54, 56–9, 105, 110, 113
    Montreal: 1976: 100–7, 109, 110, 111, 114
Osberton Horse Trials: 1969: 35; 1973: 66, 67; 1974: 81; 1975: 110; 1976: 102–3
Our Nobby, 19, 21, 28, 30, 113, 116

Page, Michael, 113
Parker, Bridget, 58, 59, 81, 113
Pasha, 33, 115, 116
Pattinson, Aly, 80, 93
Pearson, Fiona, 22
Peer Gynt, 55
Persian Holiday, 55, 61, 79, 80, 86, 95, 98, 99, 100, 103, 104, 111

Philip, HRH The Prince, Duke of Edinburgh 24, 30, 34, 36, 72, 118
Phillips, Anne, 10–11, 13, 16, 55
Phillips, Flavia, 15, 42, 110
Phillips, Peter, 11, 16, 20, 28, 29, 31–2, 43, 45
Phillips, Sarah, 10, 111
Pickles, 10, 11
Pirate, 13
Pitou, 113
Plain Sailing, 114
Playamar, 84, 99, 100, 105, 107, 114
Plumb, Michael, 83, 84, 107, 114
Pony Club, 11, 12, 13, 15, 16, 40
    championships, 12, 20, 111
    one-day event, 14, 25
Popadom, 18, 19
Portman Horse Trials, 100–1
Prickly, 108
Prior-Palmer, Lucinda, 66, 69, 88, 92, 99, 100, 103–4, 105, 106, 116
Punchestown
    World Championships: 1970: 33, 40–1, 108, 114
Purple Star, 23, 24, 25–6, 27, 35, 36–8, 111–12

Queen's Laurel, 111
Questionnaire, 19

Raisin, 108
Raleigh Trophy, 52, 60
Renwood, 110
Ribblesdale Park, 49
Riding for the Disabled Association, 93–4
Rock On, 15–21, 27, 28, 29, 30, 31, 33, 42, 48–9, 55–6, 112, 115
Rocky, 12
Roger-Smith, Althea, 19
Roger-Smith, Sarah, 36
Rome Olympics: 1960: 88
Rome Show, 62–3
Roschud, 111
Rosetime, 108
Royal Ocean, 35, 36, 112
Roycroft, Bill, 88
Rushall
    Horse Trials: 1971: 43; 1973: 62; 1975: 38
Russell, Lord Hugh, 102

Sachey, Don, 114

Sandhurst Royal Military Academy, 18, 21, 28, 79, 85–6, 95, 97
Sandringham, 11
Santa Baby, 112
Sarajevo, 113
Saumur, 30–1
Schultz, Karl, 105, 107, 114
Scott, Colonel Alec, 12, 13
Scott-Dunn, Peter, 42, 82, 84
Scottish Venture, 111
Sederholm, Lars, 36, 38
Shelly's Boy, 109
Sherbourne one-day event, 15
Sioux, 115
Sivewright, Molly, 13
Smart, John, 108
Smith, Harvey, 53, 62
Smith, Sybil, 9
Smokey VI, 81
Somerset Morn, 62
South Molton, 16, 21, 77
Sports Personality of the Year (BBC TV), 53
Sportswoman of the Year (Daily Express), 53
Sportswriters' Award, 53
Stamford, 117
Stella, 23, 111
Stevens, Stewart, 40, 52, 115
Stockenchurch one-day event, 15
Suki de Su, 111
Sutherland, Lorna, 18, 19, 22, 55
Swate, 34, 109

Talland School of Equitation, 13
Tauskey, Mary Anne, 116
Tewkesbury, 11
The Lavender Cowboy, 27
The Poacher, 22, 28, 30, 33, 39, 40, 53, 113, 114, 115, 116
Thomas, Hugh, 84, 99, 100, 103, 105, 114
Thompson, Bill, 49, 81
Three Cheers, 42, 110
Tidworth Army Horse Trials, 89, 108, 121
    1967: 17, 20; 1970: 36, 37, 38; 1972: 57; 1973: 73, 78, 79, 111; 1974: 80, 110, 111; 1975: 109; 1976: 101, 111
Tiopoletto, 108
Trim Ann, 57, 108, 109

Tucker, Mike, 12, 14, 65, 87–8, 89, 90, 92
Turnstone, 21, 22, 28
Tweseldown one-day event, 15

Upper Strata, 37, 45, 46

Vaibel, 115
Victor Dakin, 114
Vulgan, 109

Walker, Richard, 33, 36, 45, 115, 116
Warfield, 23, 34, 63
Waterstock, 36
Wayfarer II, 69, 73, 81
Weldon, Colonel Frank, 12, 13, 16,
    88, 100
Weldon, George, 12
Wellesbourne one-day event, 109
West, Debbie, 46, 52, 53, 58, 69, 115
White City, 12
Whiteley, Martin, 22, 28, 39

Wide Awake, 99, 100, 116
Willcox, Sheila, 27–8, 29, 92
Williams, Dorian, 93
Windsor
    Castle, 49
    Great Park, 10, 49, 63, 79, 96
    Royal Windsor Horse Show, 35, 63,
        112
Windspiel, 115
Wofford, James, 114
Woodland, 113
World Championships, 120
    Burghley: 1966: 117
    Punchestown: 1970: 33, 40–1, 108,
        109, 114
    Burghley: 1974: 80–4, 99, 109, 110,
        114, 117
Wramplingham one-day event: 1976:
    108
Wylye Horse Trials
    1958: 15; 1969: 108; 1973: 73, 78, 111